Unix
Made Simple

P.K. McBride

MADE SIMPLE
BOOKS

Made Simple
An imprint of Butterworth-Heinemann
Linacre House, Jordan Hill, Oxford OX2 8DP
A division of Reed Educational and Professional Publishing Ltd

ℛ   A member of the Reed Elsevier plc group

OXFORD   BOSTON   JOHANNESBURG
MELBOURNE   NEW DELHI   SINGAPORE

First published 1998
©P.K. McBride 1998

TRADEMARKS/REGISTERED TRADEMARKS
Computer hardware and software brand names mentioned in this book are protected
by their respective trademarks and are acknowledged.

British Library Cataloguing in Publication Data
A catalogue record for this book is available from the British Library

ISBN 0 7506 3571 1

Typeset by P.K.McBride, Southampton

Archtype, Bash Casual, Cotswold and Gravity fonts from Advanced Graphics Ltd
Icons designed by Sarah Ward © 1994
Printed and bound in Great Britain by Scotprint, Musselburgh, Scotland

Contents

9 Shell programming 147

Summaries 171

Index 191

Preface

Unix is a powerful, open, multi-user and multi-tasking operating system that can be run on any computer from a high-specification PC up to a mainframe. Unix-based machines can exchange data freely and be linked into networks of unrestricted size, and any computer with suitable communications software can link into a Unix system and make full use of its facilities – which is why Unix machines form the backbone of the Internet.

There are a number of versions of Unix currently in use, though fortunately, the differences between varieties are not that significant – most of the same commands are there and they mostly work in the same way. This book was writen around Unix System V, which is probably as near to a standard as you can get. Most of what is said should be equally applicable to any Unix system.

Unix was devised by programmers, for programmers, and compact power, not user-friendliness, was their prime aim. As a result, commands are terse, options legion, feedback sparse, and the potential for confusion high. In setting out to make Unix simple, I have focused on the key concepts, the essential commands and the main core of options, demonstrating them by worked practical examples.

I have written with students and new business users in mind. This book will show you how to manage and manipulate files, run applications, interact with others on your network, and set up your own part of the system the way you want it. There is also an introduction to programming in the Unix shell, for the more enterprising readers.

The Appendices contain quick reference guides to vi and to the essential Unix commands, giving for each a brief description of its purpose, major options and related commands.

Unix Made Simple replaces my earlier, and now out-of-print, book *Unix by Example*. Its material has been extensively rewritten and reorganised to suit the more accessible 'Made Simple' style.

P.K.McBride, November 1997

1 You and Unix

Computers and operating systems

Every computer system has three main components – the hardware, software and operating system.

- It's **hardware** if it hurts when you drop it on your fingers. At the heart of the system is the computer itself – the box that holds the processing and memory chips and other bits of silicon wizardry; all around it are the peripheral devices – the monitors, keyboards, disk drives, tape streamers, printers, modems and mice.

- **Software** refers to any type of computer program, but it is more commonly taken to mean application programs. These include word-processors, spreadsheets, databases and communications packages. Less obviously, applications also include programming languages, or at least, the tools that make the languages usable.

- An **operating system** is a set of programs that control the computer at the lowest level, managing access to the chips, disk drives, monitors and other devices. Without an operating system to handle all the nitty-gritty chores, using a computer would be a horrendously complex job. It also makes it possible for applications software to run on the hardware. When a word-processor wants to load a file off a disk, it doesn't need to know how the disk is organised, how far to spin it or where to put the reading head. All that can be left to the operating system.

  Operating systems smooth out the variations between different types of hardware, allowing the same program to be run across a range of computers. The part that handles the hardware is rewritten for each new machine, but the part that communicates with applications programs (and with users) remains the same.

Unix is an operating system – and more. The Unix package has a central core, or **kernel**, that controls the hardware. A **shell** program handles the interaction between you and the computer, interpreting your commands and running programs for you. There is then a large set of **commands** and **utility programs** for file-handling, directory management, text editing, messaging, and more. And all proper Unix systems have shelves of documentation that probably weigh more than their main computer!

A Unix computer system

The central processor

A typical multi-user Unix system consists of dozens – possibly hundreds – of terminals connected to a single computer. This machine can vary from a mainframe or minicomputer down to a high-power microcomputer. All that is necessary is that it should have sufficient processing power, memory and disk storage capacity to meet the needs of its users. Sometimes the computer will be *multi-tasking* – i.e. capable of doing several jobs at the same time. More commonly, it will run on a *time-share* basis. The central processor will spend a fraction of a second on a job for one user, then put it on hold – stashing it into memory – turn to the next job for a moment, then move on again. Though infinitely faster, it is not unlike a waiter looking after a dozen tables. No diner has his undivided attention, but the waiter is not missed as long as he is there when he is wanted. The computer may only be working on your job for a thousandth of a second at a time, but it will do so hundreds of times a second – faster than you can type!

On a good system, you shouldn't be aware of the fact that the computer is shared. It should be as responsive as a stand-alone desktop PC would be. This isn't always the case. If a system is getting close to its design limits, with too many users running demanding programs, or simply too many users altogether, then you may well become aware of the time-sharing aspect as the system slows down.

Terminals and peripheral devices

On most Unix systems, the terminals are usually 'dumb', consisting of a keyboard and a monitor, but with neither processing power nor memory storage of their own. In some installations you will find intelligent terminals, workstations or PCs connected into the Unix system. These are capable of doing some, or all of their own data processing. Increasingly, you will find monitors with full-colour, high-resolution graphics screen, but dumb terminals with text-only monitors are still the norm. They are quite adequate for the text and data processing that makes up so much of computing – and far cheaper.

There will usually be several printers connected into the system, to cope with both the volume and the variety of the work. High-speed printers are needed to churn out program listings and database reports for internal reference; while for those jobs that must have a more polished finish, there will be slower, high-quality machines. Printers are connected to the overall system, not to an individual terminal. This means that you can print from anywhere on the system, and so, of course, can all the other users. To prevent clashes over access, all printing is done via the central computer. When a file is sent for printing, it joins a queue on a hard disk and is passed on to the printer when its turn comes. If you have worked in the past with PCs, you will have to get used to waiting for your printouts.

Among the other peripherals devices you will almost certainly find a tape streamer, used to make backup copies of the data on the hard disks. As an ordinary user you wouldn't be expected to have do anything with this – backups are the responsibility of the system administrator. It's just reassuring to know that it is there, so that if you do erase essential files from the hard disks by mistake, you can get them back again.

Key to examples

The examples in this book use the following conventions:

login	Already displayed on the screen.
cd ..	You type in exactly as given.
filename	You type and supply the actual name.
{comment}	Don't type this, it's my comment to you.
[Return]	Press the Return or Enter key.
[a]	Press the key – lower case letter.
[Shift] – [A]	Hold **[Shift]** and press the key – upper case letter.
[Ctrl] – [D]	Hold **[Control]** and press the key – control character.
[Esc]	Press the **[Escape]** key - upper left corner.
[Backspace]	Sometimes marked **[<-Del]** or **[<-]**.

Your place in the system

Authorised users

A key difference between any multi-user system and a stand-alone personal computer is in the control of access. With a PC, anyone who can sit at the keyboard and start up the machine, has full access to the hardware and any data stored on it. (Keys and passwords may restrict the initial access, but once past those hurdles, the computer is all yours.) A multi-user system is shared, and must be shared safely. That means that users must have their own places in which to keep data safe from accidental – or malicious – corruption by others. You can't just let anyone in, and even those who are allowed into the system, cannot be given free access to do what they want, wherever they like.

To become an authorised user of the system, you must be allocated a place to store your data and given a user name and a password. (You may be given an initial password and, as you will see later, you can change it at any time.) Armed with these, you can sit down at any terminal and get access to the computer – **login** in the jargon – by typing your name and password (see page 11). At this point, the questions are, 'When you've got access, where exactly are you, and what can you do there?'

The home directory

Where you are, in terms of the system, is in your **Home** directory. This is the place on the hard disk where you will save any files that you create. Before we go any further, we should stop and look at files, hard disks and directories.

Files

A file is an organised body of information stored on a computer disk or tape, and identified by name. It may be an executable program, or a data file produced by an application. Its size may be anything from a few bytes (characters) to hundreds of Kilobytes (1K = 1024 bytes).

Directories

Even the humblest hard disk has a huge amount of storage capacity. The 200Mb (Megabyte) disks found on small PCs can store over 200 million characters. That's about 30 million words, or 300 books of this size. The hard disk capacity of a typical Unix system is measured in Gigabytes (1 Gb = 1000Mb)! Clearly, this must be organised in some way if you are ever to find any data in such a mass.

The solution is to sub-divide the storage space into directories, each one of which can have its own sub-divisions. Each directory will store the files that belong to one user, or that relate to one topic. In traditional filing terms, the hard disk is the equivalent of the room in which files are kept; the first level of directories are the cabinets, the second level are the drawers, the third are the hanging pockets. The sub-division can go further if necessary, with several folders kept in one pocket, and some folders containing batches of papers separated by divider cards. The analogy is slightly misleading as it implies that each directory is allocated a fixed amount of space, and that the process of division has to stop at some point. Neither is the case. In theory, a Unix directory can accommodate any number of files, and the sub-division can go on indefinitely. In practice, the hard disk sets an overall limit on the storage capacity, and the system administrator will keep an eye on the amount of space that each user occupies. The sub-division also comes to an end once users decide that they have enough places to store different things – at least for the time being.

The Unix directory structure is usually represented as a tree – drawn upside down. It is not a fixed structure – every organisation will develop its own – but the overall shape and certain features are common to all.

The top of the tree is identified by a single forward slash (/), and called **root**. At the first level of divisions - the filing cabinets - you will find directories called 'bin', 'tmp', 'lib', 'etc', 'usr' plus others that are specific to your installation. There will also be a number of loose files up there, for they do not have to be stored in directories. A key one here is the 'unix' file, which contains the core of the operating system.

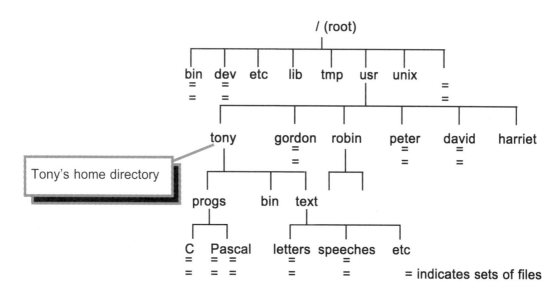

= indicates sets of files

Those standard directories serve the same purposes on all Unix systems. Their names are too terse to be really meaningful, but they may help to remind you of their contents. As an ordinary user, you are unlikely to have much to do with what's going on up there, but it is useful to have an overview of the system. Some of these directories are sub-divided, others have a single mass of files.

bin – binary files, i.e. executable programs. These include the main commands and file management utilities;

dev – devices – every terminal and other peripheral is linked to the system through a file in the dev directory;

tmp – the temporary files created by some programs;

lib – libraries of routines for some languages;

etc – files and directories for the system administrator's use;

usr – mainly applications, languages and users' directories.

We'll follow the division process further down 'usr', partly as an example of the structure, but mainly because your own directory is probably lurking somewhere in there. On a small business system, there may be no more than half a dozen or so directories – one for each user, and a few for shared files. In the example, the directories are 'tony', 'gordon', 'robin', 'peter', 'david' and 'harriet'. What happens at the next level down depends upon the user. Some users like to subdivide their areas into several levels of directories; others will stick all their files into the one place. As with a paper filing system, it depends upon the number and variety of files, and on personal attitudes to organisation.

Paths

If you look closely at the diagram, you will notice that the names of the directories are not unique. There are two named 'bin' and another two named 'etc'. This does not cause any problems. A directory is uniquely identified by its path. This tracks the sequence of directories from the root (/). Thus, the Tony's bin directory has a full path-name of '/usr/tony/bin', while the other bin at the top of the system is properly called '/bin'. Likewise, the two called 'etc' are '/etc' and '/usr/tony/text/etc'. Notice that the forward slash (/) is used both to identify the root level, and as a divider between names.

In practice, you only need to give the full path if you are elsewhere in the system. At any given point, you can identify the directories immediately below you by typing their short names. When Tony is in his home directory, '/usr/tony', he can identify his 'bin' directory by a simple 'bin'. Similarly, you can identify any that branch off further down the same part of the tree by giving the remainder of the path. So, from '/usr/tony', the etc directory would be called 'text/etc'.

Enough of theory, the best way to get to grips with directory structures and paths is to explore your own system, so let's get hands-on.

The terminal

Reading the screen

The screen keeps a record of your interaction with the system. It shows the commands that you have entered, and the responses that the central computer has sent to you. Each new line that you type, or Unix sends back, appears at the bottom of the screen, and earlier ones scroll off the top. You can't go up the screen to edit what's written there, and you can't recover those lines that have scrolled off the top.

The only part of the screen that you can edit is the line containing the prompt. Even then you are not really editing the screen itself. When you type in a command line, it is stored initially in a **buffer** (a small block of temporary memory). When you press **[Return]**, the command is passed from the buffer to the main computer, but until you do that, you can edit the buffer's contents. Which brings us to the keyboard.

Using the keyboard

Whenever you are in the shell, giving commands, and in most utility programs, the same rules apply to the way that the keyboard works.

Unix is case-sensitive

Lower case and upper case characters are different. 'fred', 'Fred' and 'FRED' are three distinct names. Unix commands, program names and most user names are written in lower case, so make sure your **[Caps Lock]** key is off. Use **[Shift]** if you ever need an upper case character.

Press [Return]

Press the **[Return]** or **[Enter]** key after you have typed in a command. Only then will the system take any notice of you.

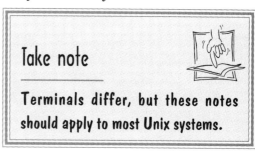

Take note

Terminals differ, but these notes should apply to most Unix systems.

x

x

Spaces matter

Whenever you type an option code or a filename after a command, you must leave a space first.

Correcting errors

If you spot an error while typing in a line, you can correct it by pressing **[Backspace]**. This deletes the last character – though the screen display may be misleading. On some systems, the cursor moves left but the character remains visible. This can be confusing. If you have Backspaced a character, it has been removed from the command line, even though you may still be able to see it. With some older systems, instead of deleting a character from the screen, the backspace adds a new one – usually #. For example, trying to give the command **date**, you mistype 'y' for 't', delete it then carry on. The resulting correct command line would appear to be '**day#te**'.

Mangled lines

As both you and the system can write to the screen at the same time, the two can sometimes get intermixed and leave you with a garbled command line. Abandon it.

Abandon line!

It is often quicker to abandon a command line and start again from scratch, than to correct it. You can abandon a line by typing [@], or [Del] or [Ctrl]-[U]. Alternatively, just press **[Return]**. The system will try to interpret your command, fail and come back with an **Unknown command**, or similar, message. There is an outside chance that in mistyping one command you will have given a different one. It's unlikely but just in case ...

Escaping from programs

If you have set a program running by accident, or are stuck in one – both of which can happen even to experienced users – you can generally escape by pressing [Del] or [Ctrl]-[D]. One or other will stop most programs.

Logging In

Before you can go any further, you'll need a terminal, and you must know your user name and password. The terminal screen should be displaying the organisation's name and a greeting, and at the bottom there should be the **login:** prompt. If you can't see this, check that the terminal is switched on, then try pressing **[Return]** a couple of times. This should make the system rewrite the screen.

Type in your user name, **[Return]** then – if required – type in your password. The characters will not be displayed on the screen, which makes for good security but frequent errors!

> **login:** *username*
> **password:** *your password*

If you mistype the password, it is probably not worth trying to correct it. Press **[Return]**, wait for the **Wrong password** message and try again.

After a successful login, you may see a message from the system administrator. This is his chance to let users know what's going on.

> The system will be shut down at 4 o'clock today for the installation of extra memory. Things should run faster tomorrow.

You may also get a message telling you that you have mail. Ignore it for the time being, but if you must read it now, turn to page 61.

The prompt

Beneath the message, you should see either a dollar ($) or percentage (%) sign. This is the **prompt**. (Yours may be something entirely different! Unix is highly adaptable and one its features that is very easy to change is the style of prompt. Your system manager may have decided to replace the single character with something more informative. Look and see what's there, then think of this whenever you see the dollar sign in the later examples.)

Whatever its style, the prompt shows that Unix is running a shell program for you, and that the shell is waiting to carry out your commands. Next to the prompt there will be an underline or a solid block – usually flashing. This is the cursor and is where text will appear when you type or when the system sends information to you.

Exploring directories

We are going to use three commands here: **ls,** which **lists** the contents of a directory; **pwd**, which gives the **p**ath to the **w**orking **d**irectory, i.e. where you are; and **cd** to **c**hange from one **d**irectory to another.

ls See what's in your directory

```
$ ls
$
```

You will probably see nothing at all – not even a message to say that the directory is empty, or that it has run the command successfully. You will only get feedback when have specifically asked for it, or when you make an error.

pwd Find out where you are in the system

```
$ pwd
/usr/staff/mac
```

That's what **pwd** shows me. What's your path? It will almost certainly start with '/usr', and include the name of the group of which you are a member. We'll climb up the tree and see who else is in the group.

cd Change directory

```
$ cd ..    { space after the cd }
$
```

A **..** (double dot) after the change directory command says 'up one level'. There's no visible effect, and no message, but that's Unix for you. It presumes that you knew what you were doing when you gave the command, and it has been performed successfully, so what is there to say? Let's check where we are and find out what's there.

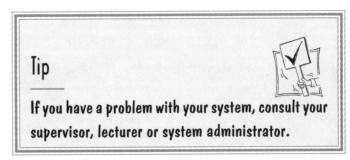

Tip

If you have a problem with your system, consult your supervisor, lecturer or system administrator.

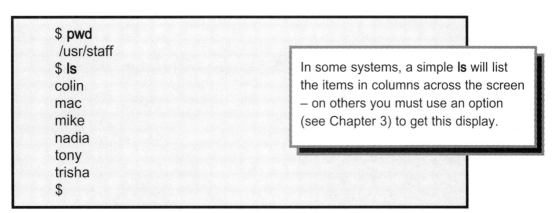

```
$ pwd
 /usr/staff
$ ls
colin
mac
mike
nadia
tony
trisha
$
```

In some systems, a simple **ls** will list the items in columns across the screen – on others you must use an option (see Chapter 3) to get this display.

pwd simply confirms where we are – it doesn't do anything useful.

ls lists the files and directories stored in the directory. In the example it lists the home directories of the staff. What do you see when you do it? Most of the names should be those of the directories of other members of your group, though there may be some files there as well.

Try to change to the directory of one of the other users. To do this, type **cd** followed by a user name from the list. You will almost certainly be greeted with a **Permission denied** message. You cannot enter other users' areas – without their express permission – any more than they can enter yours.

We'll explore directories further in the Chapter 3. Meanwhile, return to your home directory with an unqualified **cd**. If you don't say where you want to go, the system assumes you mean home.

Take note

As Unix installations vary somewhat, it is possible that some commands may have slightly different effects on your system. Don't worry about that at this stage. The reasons for the variations will become clearer later when we look at commands in more detail.

Looking around

who Who's there?

You've seen who is in your group, but who else is logged onto the system at the moment? Find out by typing **who**.

```
$ who
root      console  Mar 27 11:50
root     tty02   Mar 27 14:09
fred     tty137 Mar 27 13:39
mac      tty147 Mar 27 14:53
nadia    tty152 Mar 27 13:47
steph    tty167 Mar 27 13:43
```

For each current user, this gives the name, the terminal number (the console is the one directly attached to the computer) and the date and time when the user logged in. And when you next have an identity crisis, try this:

```
$ who am i
mac      tty147      Mar 27 14:53
```

date Finding the date and time

How does the system know when users log in? Along with most other types of computers, Unix systems have a combination clock and calendar. As long as the system administrator sets it correctly at first start-up (and adjusts it for Summer Time), it can always tell you the right time and date. If you ever want to know, just type:

```
$ date
Fri Mar 27 14:53:58 GMT 1997
```

passwd – changing your password

You can change your password at any time – and should change it regularly if you want to keep your files secure. Different systems vary slightly in their rules on passwords, but in general passwords should:

● have at least six characters, and can be longer, though only the first eight characters count;

● contain at least two letters and one number or symbol;

● be different from the login name;

● be at least three characters different from the old password.

To change the password, call up **passwd** and follow the instructions. When you type the new password it will not appear on screen, so you will be asked to retype it as a check.

```
$ passwd
New password:        {type carefully!}
Retype new password: {exactly the same again}
```

Next time you log in, use the new password. If you forget it, then all is not lost as the system administrator, or anyone else with **superuser** access, can let you in to set up a new password. (With superuser access you can do anything you like, for all files and directories are open to you. Knowledge of the root password, that grants this access, is generally a closely-guarded secret.)

Take note

When you have finished your session with Unix, you must **log out**. This frees the terminal for other users and closes the access to your part of the system. Failure to log out will allow other users to get into your directory. On some systems you can log out with the single keystroke **[Ctrl]-[D]**. On others you exit by typing:

```
$ logout
```

There might be a few seconds' delay while the system thinks about it, but you can be certain that you are logged out when the login screen comes back into view.

Help!

As a new Unix user, you will sometimes make mistakes or find yourself in situations that you do not fully understand. (Actually, that applies to almost all Unix users, new and old.) That's how it should be – if you don't make mistakes it can only be that you are not trying anything new and therefore not learning. Fortunately, there are some simple techniques that will solve most problems. First, try to identify your problem. Is it one of the 'How do I get out of this?' type, or is it a more fundamental 'What's happening?'

How do I get out of this?

You are stuck in a program which you didn't mean to get into, or have forgotten how to get out of. It is all too easy to set a program running by accident. If, for instance, you type **dc** in place of **cd**, then instead of changing directory, you will start the 'desk calculator'. (Don't let the friendly title fool you. This beast is only for mathematicians who can handle reverse Polish notation. See page 68.)

Different programs have different exit routes, but one or other of these keystrokes will work most of the time:

[Ctrl] – [D]	the normal end of session signal
[Del]	interrupts many programs
[q] or [x]	common **q**uit or e**x**it keys
[Esc] then [Shift] – [Z][Z]	the exit from vi

If none of these work, you might be tempted to turn off the terminal. Don't bother – it won't have any effect. The program will still be running when you turn it back on. Iif all else fails, you'll have to **kill** it.

Processes and how to kill them

When a program is running on the system, it is known as a **process**. The command **ps** will tell you what processes you are running at *any* terminal on the system. This is important – if your terminal is locked up in a program, you can't run **ps** from there. Go to a second terminal and login. Run **ps** with the options **-ef** to give a full list of processes, from every terminal which you are using. The simple **ps** will only tell you about the current terminal.

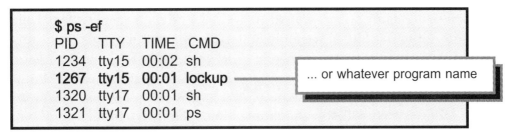

```
$ ps -ef
PID    TTY    TIME   CMD
1234   tty15  00:02  sh
1267   tty15  00:01  lockup
1320   tty17  00:01  sh
1321   tty17  00:01  ps
```

... or whatever program name

The display shows:

- the process identification numbers (PID);

- the terminal on which they are running (TTY);

- the cumulative time that the system has spent on them (TIME);

- the program or command name (CMD).

You should find that you have two **sh** or **csh** shell programs - one for each terminal, the **ps** command, and the cause of your problems. Here, the user is on terminals 15 and 17, and it is **lockup** on that is causing the trouble.

If a process appears on your **ps** list, you own it and you can **kill** it. This command takes no options, but does want a signal number. Without getting technical about it, all this means is that you have to give the number **-9** to guarantee a hit. **kill** also needs to know the PID of the process.

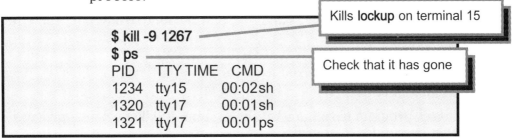

Kills **lockup** on terminal 15

```
$ kill -9 1267
$ ps
PID    TTY TIME   CMD
1234   tty15      00:02sh
1320   tty17      00:01sh
1321   tty17      00:01ps
```

Check that it has gone

If your **ps** check shows that the locking program is still running, it may just be that it took a little while to die. Wait a moment and try again. If it is still there, you must have mistyped the PID. **kill** it again.

Check back to you original terminal and you should find that you are back to your normal prompt.

What's happening?

There are many possible answers to this, and the sheer scope of Unix and the variations between installations make it impossible for any book to provide all the answers. However, there are certain common patterns and you should be able to recognise them and to know whether you can handle them yourself or need to call for help.

A suitable case

Symptom

You've just logged in and when you type in LOWER CASE it comes out in capitals, and when you type in \C\A\P\I\T\A\L\S there's a back-slash in front of the letters.

Probable cause

You had the [Caps Lock] on when you logged in. The system saw your capitals, when it had expected lower case, and decided that your terminal was one of the old ones that only uses capital letters.

Possible cure

Logout. Makes sure the [Caps Lock] is off, and login again.

Dead screens tell no tales

Symptom

The screen is totally blank and does not respond to anything you type.

Probable cause

Something's been knocked loose or turned off. Some monitors have exposed switches that can be clipped by a stray book, and cables can sometimes be snagged by people as they squeeze past – or by your own feet under the desk!

Possible cure

Check the obvious first. Is the monitor still turned on? Next look at the cable connections – but don't fiddle with them! There should be three cables plugged into the back of the terminal – all easy to identify. One will be from the keyboard; a second from the mains supply; the third carries the connection to the central computer. Do they look secure? If possible, trace the mains lead back to its socket and check that the power is turned on. If everything appears to be as it should, and there's still no joy, call for a technician.

Terminal disaster

Symptom

The screen is alive, but not well. There are garbled characters on it, and when you type, it is either ignored or garbled.

Probable cause

You have used **cat** or **vi** to display a program or data file on screen. Unlike plain text files, these are likely to contain characters outside the usual printing range.

Terminals are designed to respond to certain control characters. Character 10, for example, moves the cursor down to the next line; character 8 moves the cursor left and may (or may not, depending upon the terminal) rub out the previous letter. Other control characters will clear the screen, turn special effects on and off, and there's always at least one that will stop the terminal from responding to your typing. These are part of the ASCII set, but are not printable, i.e. they won't be seen on the screen though their effect may well be visible.

Possible cure

Turn off the terminal. Wait a few seconds while the capacitors discharge and all electrical activity ceases, then turn it back on again. The screen should be clear, and if you press [**Return**] a couple of times, your prompt will reappear.

Which program?

Symptom

You have written and (successfully) compiled a program, but when you run it, the result is completely different from what you could reasonably expect.

Probable cause

It could be simply that your program is wrong, but there's another possibility. If you call a program by the same name as an existing system utility, when you try to run it, you may well get the system program instead. The problem lies in your **PATH**, which tells Unix what directories to search and in which order. It may well look in the '/bin' and '/usr/bin' directories before it tries your current directory, and ignore your program in favour of the one it finds up there.

The **which** command will tell you which version of a program it is running, by giving you the full directory path. If you were having problems with a program called 'test', you could try:

```
$ which test
/usr/bin/test
```

This is clearly not yours!

(NB. **which** is not a standard System V program, but it is often included in the package.)

Possible cure

Use **mv** to change the name of the program and try again (see page 48). To prevent the problem recurring, you could change your PATH, so that the system tries your directories before the main */bin*. We'll return to PATHs and how to set them in Chapter 5.

No response to commands

Symptom

You cannot see the usual shell prompt ($ or whatever), but your typing appears on screen as normal. Commands do not, however, produce the desired effect.

Probable cause

You are almost certainly stuck in a program.

Possible cure

See 'How do I get out of this?' (page 16).

Crash!

Symptom

Your terminal has locked, and glancing round you see that everybody else is in the same state.

Probable cause

This is a system crash. They happen occasionally, even in the best regulated organisations.

Possible cure

Out of your hands. Go and have a cuppa while the system administrator struggles with it.

Summary

❏ Unix, like other **operating systems**, controls the computer hardware at the lowest level, as well as providing a large set of utility programs for file management and data processing.

❏ The hard disk storage is divided into **directories**, each containing a set of files (normally) belonging to one user or relating to one topic. All users have a **home directory** in which they can store their own files.

❏ On most Unix systems, users work on **dumb terminals** with text-only screens.

❏ Before you can start work, you must **log in**, giving your name and password.

❏ When exploring directories, use **ls** to see what files are there, **pwd** to find out where you are and **cd** to change to a different directory.

❏ **who** will give you a list of other users currently logged in to the system.

❏ You can – and should – use **passwd** regularly to change your password.

❏ Even experienced users get into difficulties at times. Learn to recognise the **common problems** and how to get out of them.

2 Editing text

The visual editor

vi is so-called because it is a *visual* editor – text is displayed and edited on screen. Those of you familiar with word-processors, will probably see this as being the only way to create text, but when **vi** first appeared, on-screen editing was a novelty to Unix users. Its predecessor, **ed**, was a line-based editor. With this, to edit a line of text, you had to call it up by its line number. **ed** did have some powerful editing facilities, and with practice, users could edit text very efficiently with it. **ed** is still supplied with most Unix packages and its command set is present within **vi**. Some of those commands are useful, and we will return to them at a later time. As this stage we'll stick to the core **vi** set.

Write mode and edit mode

vi has two distinct modes of operation – **write** and **edit**. When you are in **write mode** you can only write new text, and cannot alter what's already written – apart from using [Backspace] to erase the most recent characters. To delete, alter, move or otherwise edit existing text, you must go into edit mode.

In **edit mode**, the letter keys call up different functions.There are dozens of editing commands, but the few given below should be enough for the time being. Most are run from a single keypress, though two need a double click on the same key.

Take note
You may not need to read this chapter. **vi** is the most widely used of the Unix text editors, and is supplied as standard with most Unix systems, but there may be an alternative – and easier – editor in your installation. Check with your system administrator before going any further.

Instant vi

Edit keypress	Effect
[a]	Switch to Write mode, adding after cursor
[i]	Switch to Write mode, inserting before cursor
[o]	Switch to Write mode, opening a new line below
[x]	Delete character under cursor
[r] *char*	Replace character under cursor with new *char*
[d][d]	Delete whole line
[p]	Paste (deleted) line back into the text
[u]	Undo the last edit operation
[Z][Z]	Save and exit. (Note CAPITAL Zs)
[h] or [←] Left one character	
[j] or [↑]	Up a line
[k] or [↓] Down a line	
[l] or [→] Right one character	
[Esc]	Return from Write to Edit mode

> Lower and upper case have different effects. Make sure that **[Caps Lock]** is off when editing.

Getting out of trouble

Almost every key has a special function in edit mode and some call up complex routines. If you hit trouble, here are some possible solutions:

- [u] undoes the last edit – i.e. whatever you have just deleted or inserted.

- The key sequence [:] [q] [!] will usually take you right out of vi and back to your shell. When you press [:], you should see a colon appear at the bottom of the screen. When you press [q] [!] ('Quit and Abandon the edit'), 'q!' should also be displayed down there. If you don't see this, it means you have called up one of the advanced editing routines, and have to get out of that before you can do anything else.

- **[Return]** or **[Del]** will generally cancel the advanced edit routines.

If all else fails, ask your supervisor for help!

Creating a new file

We are going to create a short file called 'fox', containing the sentence 'The quick brown fox jumps over the lazy dog.' (If nothing else, it will make you find every letter on the keyboard.) Try to follow this first example as given, letter for letter – including the deliberate mistakes.

1   Call up the vi program and give a name for the file you are going to create:

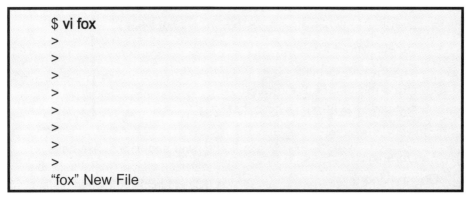

```
$ vi fox
>
>
>
>
>
>
>
>
"fox" New File
```

2   The screen will clear, with the cursor sitting up in the top left corner. The >s down the left hand side indicate empty lines. At the bottom you will see a reminder of the filename. If it is not there, it means that you forgot to specify the name when you started vi, and you will have problems later when you try to exit. If you can't see the filename, exit now by pressing [:] [q] then start again.

3   Press [a] to switch into **write** mode. Type:

The quock_

4   Stop! You have a mistype, and you've only just gone past it. Rub out back to the error by pressing [**Backspace**]. Now complete the sentence, with these errors and omissions. Press [**Return**] at the end of the line.

The quick ffox jimps ocer the lazzy dog. [Return]
          ^   ^   ^   ^

5   Press [**Esc**] to return to **edit** mode. Move the cursor, using the arrow keys or [h] [j] [k] [l], to the first 'f' of 'ffox'. Press [x] to delete it. Move on to a 'z' in 'lazzy', and press [x] again.

The quick fox jimps ocer the lazy dog.
                    ^   ^

6   Now for the mistypes. Move the cursor to the 'i' in 'jimps'. Press
     [r], for single character replace, then the correct letter 'u'. Move
     on and use [r] again to turn 'ocer' into 'over'.

The quick_fox jumps over the lazy dog.
            ^

7   One last edit. We missed out 'brown'. Move to the space after
     'quick' and press [a]. This switches you back into **write** mode.
     Type 'brown' (and a space), then press [Esc] to end writing. The
     old text will shuffle to the right to make room for the new text.

The quick brown fox jumps over the lazy dog.
[Z][Z]

8   Time to save and exit. Hold down [Shift] and press [z] twice. This
     will close down **vi** and take you back to the shell prompt. Give an
     ls command to list the files, and you should see 'fox'.

$ ls
fox

Now do it all again to fix what you have just learned. Call up **vi** and
create another one-line text file. This will take you round the keyboard
again – 'My faxed joke won a pager on a cable TV quiz show.'

$vi fax

Take it away. Remember:

[a]	to add new text;
[Backspace]	to erase mistakes in Write mode;
[Esc]	to get back to Edit;
[x]	to delete;
[r]	to replace when editing;
[Shift] – [Z][Z]	to save and exit.

Once back at the shell prompt, check your directory, and you should
find that it now contains two files.

$ ls
fox
fax

Editing an existing file

Let's get the 'fox' file back into **vi** and add a few lines. We will use some new commands and explore some key points about multi-line files.

1   Call up vi, giving it the name of the file to be edited:

    $ **vi fox**

2   The screen will clear. At the top you will see your old text and at the bottom the status line will tell you that this is 'fox' and it has 1 line and 45 characters. The cursor will be on the first character. Press **[o]** to open a new line below and switch to **write mode**. Add several lines, using **[Backspace]** to correct as you go. Press **[Return]** at the end of each line, and **[Esc]** when you have done.

> The quick brown fox jumps over the lazy dog.
> Peter Piper picked a peck of pickled peppers.
> **She sells C shells on the sea shore.**

3   Move over the text using **[h][j][k][l]** or the arrow keys. Notice that the cursor won't move into the blank area at the ends of lines. If you want to write in this area, you must press **[a]** to add at the end of the line.

4   Move the cursor to anywhere on the top line and press **[d][d]**. This will delete the line.

> The quick brown fox jumps over the lazy dog.   { **[d][d]** }
> Peter Piper picked a peck of pickled peppers.
> She sells C shells on the sea shore.

5   The line is gone – but not forgotten. Deleted text is stored in a buffer (a block of temporary memory). To put it back into the text, move the cursor to the line above where you want it to go – in this case 'She sells C shells ...' and press **[p]** (for **p**aste).

> Peter Piper picked a peck of pickled peppers.
> She sells C shells on the sea shore.   { **[p]** }
> **The quick brown fox jumps over the lazy dog.**

6   Save and exit by pressing **[Z][Z]**.

Use **vi** to write a summary of the vi commands. You can then print it out for quick reference. Which brings us to ...

Printing and printer control

In a multi-user system, users cannot send text directly for printing – a printer can only work on one item at a time. When you send a file for printing, it goes first into a queue (temporary storage on the hard disk), and is passed on to the printer when its turn comes. We will return to queue management in a moment – the important thing to realise is that there is a queue, and that there will be a delay (of a few seconds or a few minutes) before your text hits the paper.

Printing on your system

Before you try to print for the first time, check with your system administrator. As long as you are just working with files within your directories, all Unix systems are much the same, and there's little you can do that will create problems for other users. When you are interacting with external hardware, you run into variations and problems.

It is quite likely that your system has its own set of commands – custom-built shell scripts (see chapter 9) – to make printing simpler and safer. These will be two main problems that it aims solve:

● Your file must reach the right printer. The script should simplify printing, as it saves having to give the device identification, which may be necessary with a standard print command.

● It is essential to stop any non-printable files from reaching the printer. I once worked on a system that had no such trap. Several times a week a student would accidentally send a compiled (machine code) file down to the printer, and the printer would go berserk. Each fit of madness would waste yards of paper, and to restore sanity it was sometimes necessary to turn off the whole system – not just the printer! Do check with your powers-that-be.

lp

The standard command to print a file is **lp** and it must be accompanied by the name of the file, and possibly by the printer's identifier.

```
$ lp filename                    { name of file to print }
request id is pr1-5786 (1 file)  { or something similar }
```

The message 'request id ...' lets you know that the file has been placed in the queue and will be printed – sometime. The ID (pr1-5786 in the example) identifies the file in the print queue.

If your file has not been printed by the time you get to the printer, and there are others hanging around waiting for theirs, and you don't want to wait, then help is at hand. Go to your terminal and check the queue.

The print queue

Used by itself, **lpstat** tells you about your current print requests:

```
$ lpstat
pr1-6983                muggins           6625   Dec 18 11:31
```

To find out more about the queue, you must use the **-t** option. This will tell you about all the printers and the files that are in the queue:

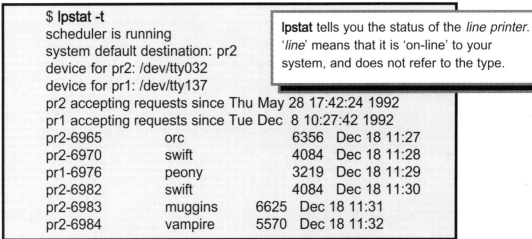

```
$ lpstat -t
scheduler is running
system default destination: pr2
device for pr2: /dev/tty032
device for pr1: /dev/tty137
pr2 accepting requests since Thu May 28 17:42:24 1992
pr1 accepting requests since Tue Dec  8 10:27:42 1992
pr2-6965        orc                 6356   Dec 18 11:27
pr2-6970        swift               4084   Dec 18 11:28
pr1-6976        peony               3219   Dec 18 11:29
pr2-6982        swift               4084   Dec 18 11:30
pr2-6983        muggins        6625   Dec 18 11:31
pr2-6984        vampire        5570   Dec 18 11:32
```

lpstat tells you the status of the *line printer*. *'line'* means that it is 'on-line' to your system, and does not refer to the type.

And there are you, muggins, stuck almost at the end of the queue! You can be patient, or you can cancel the print request and try again later.

cancel

To cancel a print-job, all you need to know is its ID. This is the one that was displayed when you first sent the file for printing. In case that is no longer visible on your screen, it is also displayed in the left-hand column of the **lpstat** output. The command is a plain:

```
$ cancel pr2-6983     { or whatever ID number }
```

Filenames

Unix is easy-going in its rules about filenames, but there are certain conventions. A filename is normally a single word, or a name and a suffix, separated by a dot (.) e.g. 'chap1.txt', 'stock.c', 'chap1.bak', 'mytext'.

The **suffix** is used to identify the type of file, for the benefit of the user or of an application program. (It has no special meaning to Unix.) You might chose to label text files with a '.txt', and backup copies with a '.bak' suffix. C programs should have a '.c' suffix, mainly because most C compilers insist that the program files have '.c' at the end.

The **maximum length** of filenames varies between systems, but is typically 14 characters. These can be almost any characters, though some are best avoided. Use letters and digits only, and you won't go far wrong.

If you want to have **more than one word** in the filename, use the underscore (_) or dot (.) as a separator. Don't use spaces, as Unix treats spaces as marking the ends of words.

The symbols * ? [ ] - ( ) \ ' " ; : ! have special meanings and should not be used. If you start a name with a dot, it will not normally be displayed by **ls**, which can be useful if you want to tuck a file out of the way.

Make your filenames meaningful. They should remind you instantly of the contents or purpose of the file. Keep them short if possible. Long names give more opportunities for typing errors.

Be consistent in your use of **upper** and **lower case**, as Unix treats them as being different. 'MYPROG' is not the same as 'myprog'.e.g.

stock92.data	good name for this year's stock records
letter	poor – O.K. by Unix, but meaningless
john.memo	could be more informative and...
John.memo	... you'll confuse it with this one
.hidden	good if you want to keep it discrete
jones_may4.let	couldn't that be shorter?

Summary

- [ ] **vi** is the standard 'visual editor' found on most Unix systems. Though crude compared to current word-processors, it allows quick and efficient editing, once you have learnt its limited command set.

- [ ] vi has two modes or working. You must go into **write** mode to add new text, and into **edit** mode to move around existing text.

- [ ] To **create a new text file**, or edit an existing one, start vi and give the name of the file.

- [ ] To **print a file** you can use the **lp** command (though an alternative may have been set up for your particular system).

- [ ] If you want to check your place in the **printer queue**, use **lpstat**. You can **cancel** a print request if you are too far down the queue and can't wait!

- [ ] There are a **few rules governing filenames**, but the most important one is 'Make it meaningful!'

3 Directories and files

The directory tree

Earlier, I defined a **file** as an organised body of information stored on a disk, and a **directory** as a place on the disk where files can be stored. They are good working definitions and probably the best way to think about them, but they don't tell the full story. In Unix, a directory is a file – albeit a special sort of file. The operating system sees a directory not as space on the disk, but an index to where files are stored. When you change directory, you are turning to a new place in the index.

In practice, you don't need to worry much about this distinction, but it does have a couple of important considerations. It means that the same rules apply to directory names as to filenames, and that directories and files are listed together when you type **ls**. It's not difficult to tell which is which, as you will see when we look at the **ls** options – but to do that properly, we need to find some directories with a bit of variety in them. So first, let's go exploring.

Below is a simplified view of a typical structure – simplified by giving only the sub-divisions of one directory at each level. It will be useful at this stage to draw a similar diagram for your system. Apart from being a good exercise, it will produce a reference map for later use.

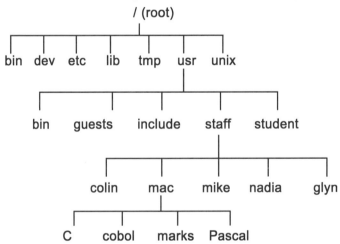

1   Start by making sure that you are in your own directory. Type **pwd** to get the path. If your user name is not the last item in the path name, you have strayed from home. Get back to your directory by typing **cd**.

2 You are going to move up a level, check the path and list the directory contents. The screen display should be like this.

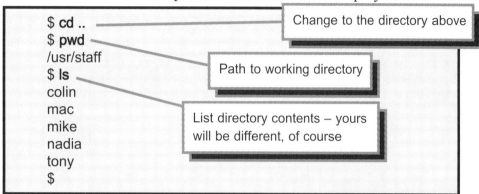

```
$ cd ..                    Change to the directory above
$ pwd
/usr/staff
$ ls                       Path to working directory
colin
mac
mike                       List directory contents – yours
nadia                      will be different, of course
tony
$
```

3 Repeat that same sequence of commands - **cd .. pwd ls** - to work back up to the top of the tree, looking around you as you go.

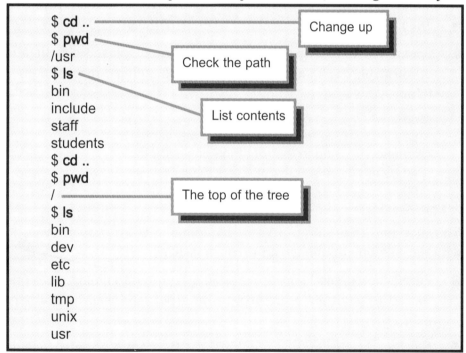

```
$ cd ..                    Change up
$ pwd
/usr                       Check the path
$ ls
bin
include
staff                      List contents
students
$ cd ..
$ pwd
/                          The top of the tree
$ ls
bin
dev
etc
lib
tmp
unix
usr
```

4 When the path is a single slash (/) you have reached the top. At that level, you should find the same core of directory contents in every Unix system. There will always be 'bin', 'dev', 'etc', 'lib', 'tmp' and 'usr' directories – and the 'unix' program file.

What's in these directories? Why not go and look? Some of them should be open for you to view.

5   To change into a directory that appears in the list, just type the name after **cd** - don't forget the space after the command word.

```
$ cd bin
$ ls
acctcom
aomlogin
...
...
who
write
```

There's an awful lot of stuff in the 'bin', isn't there! These are the main command and utility programs. You might have seen **login**, **pwd** and **ls** as they shot by. (You'll learn how to control these displays shortly.)

6   Spend a little time moving around the directories to get the feel of the structure. Use these **cd** options, changing directory names to suit your system:

cd ..	up one level
cd /	leap to the root from anywhere
cd /etc	up to the root then down to etc
cd dir1/dir2	down through dir1 to dir2
cd ../..	up two levels
cd	back to your Home directory

You may find that some of your **cd** commands are not obeyed, in which case you should see an error message:

● **Permission denied** shows that you attempted to change into one owned by another user, or into one that is closed to ordinary users.

● **Not found** tells you that you have got the name (or path) wrong. On some systems, if you type a near-miss (the odd letter wrong), the system will try and guess what you meant.

```
$ cd bim       { ends in 'm' }
cd bin? y      { or 'n' if you didn't mean that one }
```

36

ls - list directory contents

A plain **ls** gives a names-only display, in one long list. Sometimes that is not enough – and sometimes it is too much. **ls**, like many Unix commands, has several options, each identified by a single letter. To use an option, write a dash then the letter after the command, e.g.

> **ls -l**   {specifying the long directory listing}

Note that space after **ls**. Miss it out and the system won't know what you're talking about. Take care with cases. Some options are identified by capitals, others by lower case. **ls -L** is quite different from **ls -l**.

ls has some two dozen options. These are the most useful ones.

ls -l The long list

Let's try the long list and find out more about how files are stored. We need a directory with something in it – the root will do nicely.

```
$ cd /                                    Go to the root
$ ls -l          Long list
total 495
drwxr-xr-x   2    bin    bin    1504    Apr 13 14:37   bin
-rw-r--r--   1    root   sys    19244   Apr 13 12:15   boot
drwxr-xr-x   4    root   sys    1424    Apr 13 13:13   dev
drwxr-xr-x   7    root   sys    1488    Apr 23 00:08   etc
drwxrwxrwx   3    bin    bin    384     Apr 13 13:48   lib
drwxrwxrwx   3    root   root   80      Apr 23 02:41   tmp
-rw-r--r--   1    root   sys    204975  Apr 13 12:15   unix
drwxr-xr-x   19   bin    bin    320     Apr 23 00:08   usr
```

Compact, coded information like this may be a bit forbidding at first glance, but it makes sense when you start to break it down. I'll head up the listing and work through the columns one at a time.

permissions	links	owner	group	size	date	time	name
drwxr-xr-x	2	bin	bin	1504	Apr 13	14:37	bin
-rw-r--r--	1	root	sys	19244	Apr 13	12:15	boot

The first character indicates the type of file. '**d**' stands for directory; '-' is a normal file.

Elsewhere in the system, particularly in the '/dev' directory you will find '**b**' which marks block storage media – the hard and floppy disks;

37

and '**c**' for character-based files, i.e. the terminals. (Yes, terminals are also files in Unix, but don't let that bother you.)

Permissions

The **permissions** tell you who can do what to the file. There are three sets, each of three characters. The first set are the permissions enjoyed by the owner (**user**) of the file, the second by other members of his **group**, and the last by all the **others** on the system.

user	group	others		
rwx	r-x	r-x	....	bin
rw-	r--	r--	....	boot

The **access modes** are:

r   read – and display or copy it, but without changing it in any way;

w   write – and edit, rename and delete;

x   execute a program, or have full access to a directory.

We'll return to **chmod** on page 66.

Links

The **links** figure tells you how many directories are linked to that file. Ordinary files will normally have only one link. Directories have at least two – one to themselves and one to the directory above. Anything higher normally means that the directory has sub-directories.

Owner and group

These should be obvious. If you find any in your directory that do not list you as the owner, then ask your system administrator to investigate!

File size

The size of a file is measured in bytes. If you need to reduce your use of storage space, it's worth knowing which files take up most space.

Date and time

These refer to when the file was last updated. When the system administrator is running the backup routine, the system will use this to pick out those files that have been changed since the last backup.

Other ls options

ls -C Column-wise list

This lists files, by name only, in columns – useful where there are lots. Try it in the '/bin'.

```
$ cd /bin
$ ls -C
acctcom   chown    du       kill     mail     pdp11    size     u3b
aomlogin  cmp      dump     l        make     ps       sleep    u3b10
....
chgrp     diff     ipcrm    lx       od       sed      tty
chmod     dirname  ipcs     m68k     passwd   sh       u370
```

ls -F list with Filetype

This also lists in columns, but adds a file type indicator at the end. '*' marks executable programs, '/' a directory. The 'bin' isn't very interesting for this – they are all executable. Try your 'etc' directory:

```
$ cd /etc
$ ls -F
add.hd*      ff*        layout*    mvdir*     swap*
admcrontab   filesave*  layouts/   ncheck*    sys.start*
....
```

Your display will be different, but most should be executable* programs, with some directories/ and (unmarked) data files.

ls -a list all

This lists all files, including those starting with a dot, which are normally ignored. Try it in any directory and you will see that the first two files in the list are always . (dot) and .. (dot dot). dot refers to the directory itself; dot dot has the connection back to the parent directory – the next one up the tree.

ls -t List by time

This lists files in date order, latest first, rather than in alphabetical order. This is very handy for tracking down the files that you were using in your last working session if you have forgotten their names.

Combining options

Options may be combined by writing the code letters in a continuous list after the dash. The order is not important. When you want full information about a directory try this:

```
$ls -alF ─────────────────────────────── all, long and File types
total 495
drwxr-xr-x   9    root    sys     224        Apr 23 11:09 ./
drwxr-xr-x   9    root    sys     224        Apr 23 11:09 ../
drwxr-xr-x   2    bin     bin     1504       Apr 13 14:37 bin/
-rw-r—r—     1    root    sys     19244      Apr 13 12:15 boot
drwxr-xr-x   4    root    sys     1424       Apr 13 13:13 dev/
drwxr-xr-x   7    root    sys     1488       Apr 23 00:08 etc/
drwxrwxrwx   3    bin     bin     384        Apr 13 13:48 lib/
drwxrwxrwx   3    root    root    80         Apr 23 02:41 tmp/
-rw-r—r—     1    root    sys     204975     Apr 13 12:15 unix
drwxr-xr-x   19   bin     bin     320        Apr 23 00:08 usr/
```

Similarly, for a Column-wise, time-order listing you would use:

```
$ ls -Ct
```

Selective lists

The option codes determine **how** files are listed. You can give **ls** information to determine **which** files are listed. Give it the name of a directory and **ls** will list its contents, e.g. to get a long list of **/tmp**:

```
$ ls -l /tmp
```

Give it the name of a file, and **ls** will list it – and no other – if that file is in the current directory. Does 'fred' exist?

```
$ ls fred
fred: Not Found
```

You can check for several files at a time by giving their names in a list.

```
$ ls fox fax fred
fox
fax
fred: Not found
```

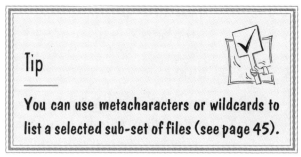

Tip

You can use metacharacters or wildcards to list a selected sub-set of files (see page 45).

Making directories

If you are going to use your Unix system properly, you should organise your files into a set of sub-directories, one for each category of file. How you define a category is up to you, and will depend upon what you are doing. As a student, you might have a directory for each module of your course; in a business environment, files might be organised by department, by project or by type of client. This does not have to be done immediately. You can make or remove directories at any time, and it's simple enough to move files from one to another. But you do need to make a couple of directories now – partly for practice, partly because you'll need them to follow later examples.

mkdir – make directory

First, go home with **cd**. To make a directory, use the command **mkdir**, giving it the new name. We'll make two, called 'examples' and 'temp'.

```
$ mkdir examples
$ mkdir temp
```

As usual, Unix doesn't bother to tell you when it has successfully performed a command. To see for yourself that the directories have been created, call up **ls**. Their names will appear along with your files.

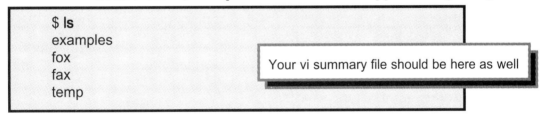

```
$ ls
examples
fox
fax
temp
```

Your vi summary file should be here as well

rmdir – remove directory

'examples' will be for storing files created in later examples. 'temp' is very temporary – it is there to give you a chance to get rid of it. The command to remove a directory is **rmdir**. You must give it the directory name, and it will only be performed if the directory is empty.

```
$ rmdir temp
```

Sorry. We'll shortly be needing a directory called 'temp' after all. You know how to set it up.

Paths, files and directories

To identify a directory or a file that is in your current directory, i.e. where you are at the time, all you need is its name. If you want one that is elsewhere in the system, you must also specify its **path**. This can be done in two ways – either the full path, starting at the root, or by tracking from where you are now to where the file is kept.

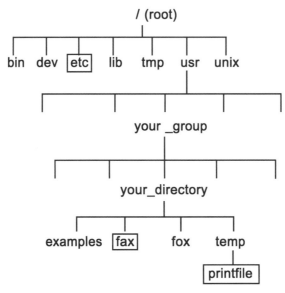

Assume that you are currently in your 'examples' sub-directory and you are interested in the 'etc' directory and in two files – 'fax' in your main directory, and 'printfile' in your temp sub-directory. Using the paths from the root, these can be identified by:

```
/etc
/usr/your_group/your_directory/fax
/usr/your_group/your_directory/temp/printfile
```

Tracking from your current position the paths become:

```
../../../../etc       { up 4 levels and down into etc }
../fax                { up one level and there it is }
../temp/printfile     { up one level, across and down again }
```

With a nearby directory, it is simpler to track a route from where you are. With a distant one, it is simpler to work from the root.

Copying files

The huge advantage that computer files have over paper-based ones is that it is so easy to keep them organised. A moment's thought and a few seconds' typing is all it takes to copy, move, rename or remove a file – or a whole set of them.

cp – copy a file

The **cp** command can be used in two ways – to create a second, renamed, copy of a file, or to copy a file into another directory. For operations of the first type, Unix needs two items of information – the name of the original file and the name that the copy is to be called. These items – *arguments* in the jargon – are written after the command, separated by spaces.

Create a new copy of a file

    $ cd   { go home }
    $ cp fox fox.bak

This creates a backup copy of your fox file, and puts it in your current directory as you haven't said otherwise.

    $ cp fox examples/fox.bak

As the path is included in the name, this **cp** will create the copied file in the specified directory, and call it 'fox.bak'.

Copy a file into a new directory

    $ cp fox examples

This time the directory is specified, but there is no name for the new file. The copy will be placed in 'examples' but still called 'fox'. We are now using **cp** in its second way, and there is an important variation here. For cross-directory copying, the command has the form:

    cp filelist destination

The *filelist* can be a set of named files or a wildcard expression (see page 45). The *destination* is a simple directory name.

    $ cp fox fax fix temp
    fix: Not found

When Unix performs this command, it will check that the last argument, 'temp', is a valid directory name, then work through 'fox', 'fax' and 'fix' attempting to copy each into 'temp'.

```
$ cp temp/* examples
```

Here the wildcard asks for all files in the 'temp' directory to be copied into 'examples'.

Please run through these examples, if you haven't already done so. You will need the directory structure and contents shown here in later examples. (Any extra files won't matter.)

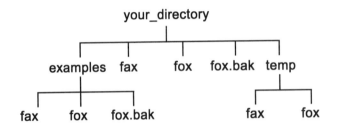

Take note

You cannot change filenames when doing a multiple copy – not even to add a '.bak' to the end of them all.

Wildcards and filenames

Wildcards – more correctly called **metacharacters** – are characters that can stand for any others, just as wildcards (or jokers) can in a pack of playing cards.

* stands for any set of characters;

? replaces any single character;

[] enclose a set of alternative characters.

Use these in a situation where Unix is expecting a filename – or a set of filenames – and it will take the wildcard expression and expand it into a list of names. Combine them with real characters to specify limited sets of names, e.g.

Expression	Expands into..
f*	Any name starting with 'f'
*.txt	Any name with '.txt' at the end
.*	Any name starting with '.'
f?x	'fox', 'fax', and any similar
????	Any name of four characters
f[ao]x	Either 'fax' or 'fox'
jan[1-5]	'jan1', 'jan2', 'jan3', 'jan4', 'jan5'

The brackets are probably the least used of the wildcards. You can bracket either:

● a fixed list of characters - [abc] standing for either a, b or c;

● or a set described by its limits - [a-e] stands for a, b, c, d or e.

Practise using wildcards with **ls** - you can see instantly whether you are forming the expressions correctly, and you can't do any damage!

The examples below are based on a directory containing these files and sub-directories:

.login	.profile	chap1.bak	chap1.txt	chap2.bak	chap2.txt
chp3.txt	examples	fax	fax.bak	fox	fred
temp	w	wholist	x	yz	

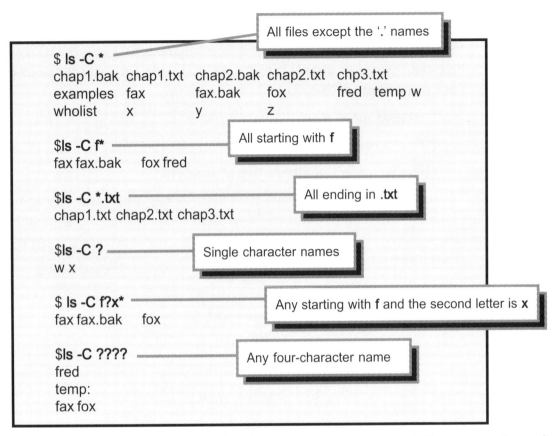

```
$ ls -C *
chap1.bak  chap1.txt  chap2.bak  chap2.txt  chp3.txt
examples   fax        fax.bak    fox        fred  temp w
wholist    x          y          z
```
All files except the '.' names

```
$ls -C f*
fax fax.bak    fox fred
```
All starting with **f**

```
$ls -C *.txt
chap1.txt chap2.txt chap3.txt
```
All ending in **.txt**

```
$ls -C ?
w x
```
Single character names

```
$ ls -C f?x*
fax fax.bak    fox
```
Any starting with **f** and the second letter is **x**

```
$ls -C ????
fred
temp:
fax fox
```
Any four-character name

In that last example, the expression generated the name of a sub-directory, and **ls -C temp** command lists its contents.

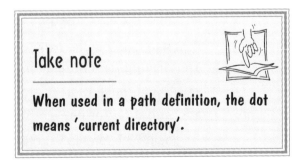

Take note

When used in a path definition, the dot means 'current directory'.

rm – remove a file

Use with care! **rm** works is strictly one-way. If you remove a file by mistake, you can only recover it if your system administrator has it on the back-up tapes. As back-ups are normally done overnight, there's little hope of recovering a file created and removed on the same day.

The command takes a single file, a list or a wildcard expression as its argument. Try these examples – note the changes of directory.

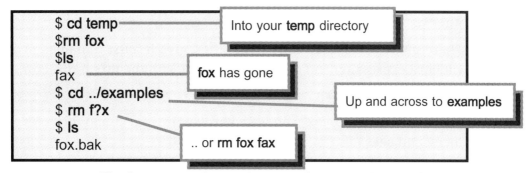

```
$ cd temp                    Into your temp directory
$rm fox
$ls
fax                          fox has gone
$ cd ../examples
$ rm f?x                     Up and across to examples
$ ls
fox.bak                      .. or rm fox fax
```

The **ls** commands are there to show you that the files really have been removed. You only get feedback if you ask it to remove a directory or a non-existent file. Watch what happens when you try it – and don't miss out the line that copies everything from your home directory into 'examples'. You are about to wipe the directory clean, and without the copies, you'll lose your hard-won files.

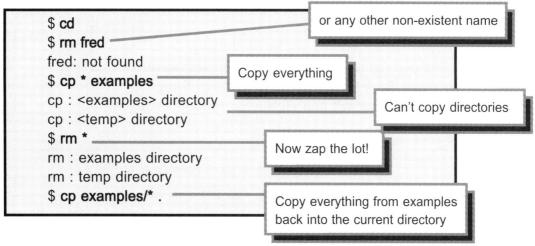

```
$ cd                         or any other non-existent name
$ rm fred
fred: not found
$ cp * examples              Copy everything
cp : <examples> directory
cp : <temp> directory        Can't copy directories
$ rm *
rm : examples directory      Now zap the lot!
rm : temp directory
$ cp examples/* .            Copy everything from examples
                             back into the current directory
```

Never do **rm *** again unless you are absolutely sure that you mean it!

mv – move or rename a file

Using **mv** has exactly the same effect as a **cp** followed by a **rm**. The rules for its use are therefore much the same.

If you are using it to rename files, they must be processed one at a time as the old and new names must be individually specified.

$ mv fox quickbrown

The file 'fox' has now had its name changed to 'quickbrown' but is otherwise exactly the same.

Where **mv** is being used to relocate files, give it a list of names or a wildcard expression and end the command with the target directory.

$ mv fax quickbrown temp

This will move both 'fax' and 'quickbrown' to your 'temp' directory. Check and see:

```
$ ls    { in your Home directory }
fox.bak    { you may have more here }
$cd temp
$ ls
fox  quickbrown  { and in here }
$ cd    { back Home again }
$ mv temp/* . { move them back home }
$ mv * temp   { and shift the lot out again }
mv : <examples> directory
mv : <temp> directory
$
```

As usual, Unix only tells you about the things it can't do. Look into 'temp' and you will find all the old Home files there.

Other commands

cat – display text file

cat will display a text file for reading, though not for editing.

$ cat fox
The quick brown fox jumps over the lazy dog.

cat can be used for creating and processing files – see pages 55 and 114.

pg – paged display of text files

If a text file has more than twenty or so lines, a simple **cat** will scroll the top lines up and off the screen. Use **pg** for longer files.

pg pauses at the end of each screenful and waits for your command. These include facilities for searching for text items and for moving within the text to selected lines. We'll return to these in Chapter 7. For most of us, for most of the time, these are only commands we need:

[Space Bar] display next page

[Q] or [Del] quit

[H] display command summary

You will need a good-sized text file to test this – is your vi summary longer than one page, or do you have anything else suitable?

$ pg visummary

file – what type is it?

The **file** command looks at a file, or set of files, and takes an educated guess as to the nature of the file(s). Try it on a single file and on the whole directory:

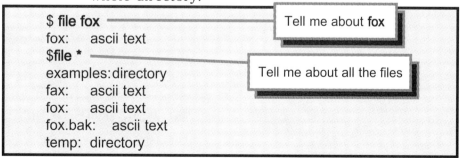

```
$ file fox                          Tell me about fox
fox:    ascii text
$file *                             Tell me about all the files
examples:directory
fax:    ascii text
fox:    ascii text
fox.bak:   ascii text
temp: directory
```

file can recognise executable programs and data files, and can distinguish between different types of text files – shell scripts and programs in other languages, English and plain ASCII text. It makes the odd mistake, but is nevertheless a quicker way of checking a file's type than using **cat** or **pg** to view it on screen. It is also a lot safer. If you use either of these to display a program or data file, the command will cheerfully send all the characters to the screen, including those that are non-printable. You can fairly guarantee that at least one of these will be a control character that renders the terminal unusable.

du – disk usage

Disk space is not unlimited. Find out from your system administrator how much space you can use, then check your disk usage with **du**.

```
% du
42      ./PASCAL/
14      ./Mail/
20      ./temp/
24      ./learning/
28      ./language/pascal/
12      ./language/vi/
40      ./language/
160     ./
```

This shows the disk usage of each directory, and the overall total, with the values given in **blocks**. Each of these will be 512 bytes, so divide by 2 to get the total K. In this example, the user is occupying 80K of disk space. If you find that you are at – or over – your limit, the **du** breakdown will show you where to try first when looking for savings.

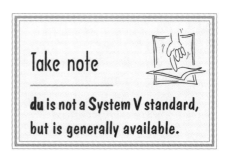

Take note

du is not a System V standard, but is generally available.

Good housekeeping

Small is beautiful

It's easier to find a file in a directory where the **ls** list fits on one screen than in one where the list fills several screens. But how many is a screenful? With **ls -C** you can fit over a 100 on a screen; with **ls -l** you can only fit around 24. If the name alone is enough to identify a file, then the compressed listing will do. If you want more information then you will use the long listing, and will need to keep the numbers down.

Everything in its place

Have separate directories for each area of your work. If you create a file in the wrong directory - move it. If a directory becomes over-full, set up new sub-directories and move sets of files into them.

But don't over-organise

You will find it easier to find files and move between directories if you have only one set, all branching off from your main directory. A complex tree structure, containing directories within directories, sub-divided to the umpteenth level, can become an impassable maze.

Group by name

Make full use of suffixes. Files marked '.memo', '.text', '.bak', '.data' are easily recognised and can be copied and moved in bulk with wildcards. But take the grouping beyond that and get the same bulk file management by starting all related files in the same way. For instance, use a client's initials to prefix the memos, letters and reports relating to that person.

Keep it clean

Remove unwanted files as you go along, rather than letting them clutter up your directories.

When in doubt, don't!

If you are not certain that a file is unwanted, rather than remove it completely, move it into a temporary directory. Check this from time to time, making a note of the files' dates. Any that have not been touched recently are presumably unwanted and can be removed.

Summary

❏ The directory structure is usually referred to as a **tree** – though the 'root' is at the top! A directory can hold sub-directories, each of which can be sub-divided *ad infinitum*.

❏ The **ls** command will **list the files in a directory**. Its options let you control how much detail is displayed, and the style of display.

❏ You can **create new directories** (within your home directory) using **mkdir**.

❏ **Directories can be removed**, once they are empty, with **rmdir**.

❏ A **path** describes the place of a file or directory within the system.

❏ You can create **copies of files** in other directories, or in the same directory but with a different filename.

❏ **Wildcards** allow you to select groups of files with related names.

❏ Use **rm** to **remove an unwanted file** – or a wildcard-selected set.

❏ Sets of files can be **moved**, and single ones moved or **renamed** with **mv**.

❏ If you want to **view a file**, use **cat** or **pg** – pg is better for files longer than one screenful.

❏ **file** will tell you the nature of the files in a directory.

❏ **du** will tell you how much disk space you are using.

❏ For tidy, well-organised directories, follow the '**good housekeeping**' tips.

4 Working on the system

Manuals and the on-line manual

The manuals supplied with Unix systems are very thorough, but heavy going even for experienced users. This is inevitable as the Unix commands and utilities are so complex and have so many options, that the documentation has to be concise if it's to be kept to a reasonable size. As it is, there will be up to a dozen hefty loose-leaf tomes. Two of the manuals are of interest to the ordinary user.

- The **User Guide** gives an overview of the system, tutorials in the use of the editors **ed** and **vi**, and on shell programming. If you want to be a Unix programmer, you will need this.

- The **User Reference** describes the commands and utilities. Turn to this if you have problems, or when you have mastered the basics and want to start exploring the system. If the book is not accessible, you can read the same information on your screen.

man – the on-line manual

To read up on any command, type **man** and the command name. The information is laid out in a standard format:

- **Name** and brief definition
- **Synopsis** of usage with list of options, e.g. with **ls** it looks like this:

    ls [-abcCdfFgilLmnopqrRstux] [filenames]

    Anything in square brackets is optional. Where there is a list of option letters bracketed together, any combination can be used.

- **Description** of how it works and what it does – this is sometimes very clear, but can be either terse or technical or both
- **Options** describe the effect of each
- **Examples** show how the command is used and covers key options
- **Files** lists the files used by, or created by, the command
- **See Also** lists related commands and relevant sections of the Reference Manual.

There may also be sections headed **Bugs**, if any are known; **Diagnostics**, where there are error messages; and **Warnings**, where a misused command may have particularly unwanted effects.

Input and output

Unix assumes, unless told otherwise, that the input comes from the keyboard and the output goes to the monitor. This is all quite reasonable and shouldn't cause any raised eyebrows. The important point is that Unix is just as happy to accept the input from a file and to send the output to a file. This is known as **I/O** (Input/Output) **redirection** and is managed via the symbols < and >.

Output redirection

Try this. It will redirect the output of **ls** into a file called 'lsfile'. The space between the redirector '>' and the filename is optional, but makes the line more readable.

        $ ls -l > lsfile

The directory contents are now on file and can be printed or read on screen with **cat** or **pg**. Use redirection like this whenever you want to retain a permanent record of a program's output.

Redirection can also be used with **cat** in two different and interesting ways. In its simple version, this command will display one or more files on screen.

        $ cat fox fax
        The quick brown fox jumped over the lazy dog
        My faxed joke won a pager in the cable tv quiz show

Redirect the output and it will join the source files together to create a new file. This is the simplest way to merge text files.

        $cat fox fax > combined
        $ ls
        combined   examples fax fox fox.bak   temp
        $cat combined
        The quick brown fox jumped over the lazy dog
        My faxed joke won a pager in the cable tv quiz show

Instant files

If you don't give **cat** a source file, then it will take its input from the keyboard. This may not appear to be a lot of use, but combined with output redirection it can be a quick way of creating short files.

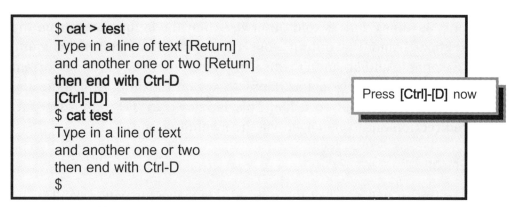

```
$ cat > test
Type in a line of text [Return]
and another one or two [Return]
then end with Ctrl-D
[Ctrl]-[D]  ————————————————————  Press [Ctrl]-[D] now
$ cat test
Type in a line of text
and another one or two
then end with Ctrl-D
$
```

You can erase mistakes while you're on the same line, but you cannot edit a line after you have pressed [Return]. So what use is such a rough and ready means of file-creation? Well, it's quick, and if what you are writing is very short or the odd error is immaterial, then it can be handy. There are two situations in particular where you might use **cat** instead of **vi** – writing memos to send in the mail (see page 61) and writing simple shell scripts (see Chapter 9).

If you use a double >>, instead of a single redirector, the output (from file or keyboard) is **appended** to the end of an existing file. Try it:

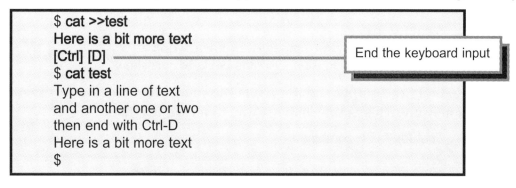

```
$ cat >>test
Here is a bit more text
[Ctrl] [D]  ————————————————————  End the keyboard input
$ cat test
Type in a line of text
and another one or two
then end with Ctrl-D
Here is a bit more text
$
```

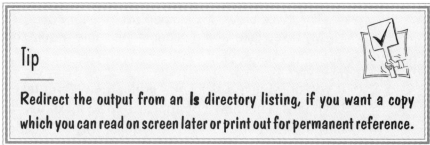

Tip

Redirect the output from an **ls** directory listing, if you want a copy which you can read on screen later or print out for permanent reference.

Input redirection

To demonstrate **Input redirection**, we need a program or command that takes keyboard input, and everything we've covered so far either takes no input at all or works on files. There's one exception that we could use – the **passwd** command (though this is a bit of a forced example!).

When you run this, your conversation with the computer will go something like this:

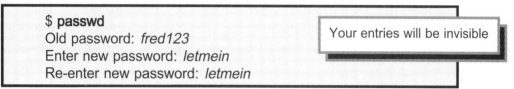

```
$ passwd
Old password: fred123                    Your entries will be invisible
Enter new password: letmein
Re-enter new password: letmein
```

There are some variations of this, so run it first to find out exactly how yours works. Make a note of the keystrokes that you make – including [Return] presses. Now write these into a file, using **cat**:

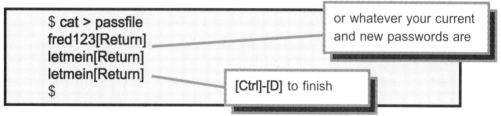

```
$ cat > passfile              or whatever your current
fred123[Return]               and new passwords are
letmein[Return]
letmein[Return]
$                   [Ctrl]-[D] to finish
```

We can now use Input redirection to pass this keystroke sequence to the **passwd** program.

```
$ passwd < passfile
```

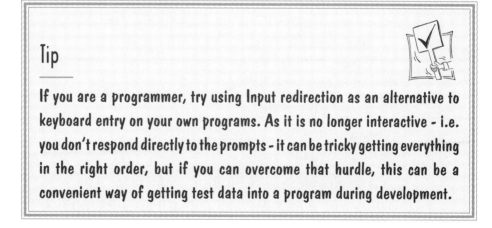

Tip

If you are a programmer, try using Input redirection as an alternative to keyboard entry on your own programs. As it is no longer interactive - i.e. you don't respond directly to the prompts - it can be tricky getting everything in the right order, but if you can overcome that hurdle, this can be a convenient way of getting test data into a program during development.

Pipelines

One of the features of Unix that gives it such power, is the ease with which commands and utility programs can be linked together. The output of one program can be the input for another – directly, without having to go through an intermediate file. In the jargon, you are setting up a **pipeline**, or more briefly **pipe**, and the symbol that links the commands is the vertical bar '|'. (This is usually located on the backslash key.)

Suppose that you wanted to examine the '/bin' directory. The full listing is far too long to fit on screen. You could redirect the output from **ls -l** to a file, then display that with **pg**, or you could pipe it with:

$ **ls -l /bin | pg**

/bin directory ▶ | ls -l | ▶ raw listing ▶ | pg | ▶ paged listing

Pipes are a key part of Unix's building-block approach. Instead of having a few highly complex programs to handle file management and text-processing, it has a very large set of single-purpose utilities. These are often referred to as **filters**, where they take a stream of data, perform some process on it and pass on the result – either to the screen, a file, or another filter. By linking them together through pipes, you can perform an almost infinite variety of sophisticated processing tasks. Paged directory listing is a simple, though useful, example of what can be done.

A development from the simple pipe is the **tee** – the T-junction in the plumbing analogy. This splits the output from a command, sending it to the screen, as normal, with a copy going either to a file or to the next command in the pipeline. It cannot be used as a stand-alone command, but only as a pipe fitting.

$ **ls -l | tee lsfile**

This will give you a screen display of the directory list, and create a file called 'lsfile'.

It is a valuable facility for programmers, as it allows them to collect a copy of their screen displays in a file, while viewing them on screen.

There are two **tee** options.

-i makes it ignore interrupts, and is rarely necessary;

-a appends the output to an existing file, rather than overwriting it. For example, we could redirect today's date to a file, then append the current directory listing to it:

```
$ date > today
$ ls -l | tee -a today
```

There are three other possible pipeline connectors.

^ (carat) is a straight alternative – the effects are identical.

&& (and) the following command is only executed if the preceding one is executed successful;

| | (or) the following command is only run if the earlier one fails.

(Look out for other examples of pipelines further on in the book.)

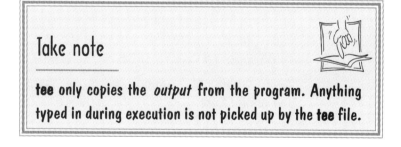

Take note

tee only copies the *output* from the program. Anything typed in during execution is not picked up by the **tee** file.

Multi-tasking!

Lists of commands

If you want to run through a set of commands, one immediately after the next, you can write them into a single command line. Use a semicolon to separate each command from the next. It won't save you any time or typing, but at least you won't have to wait for each to finish before giving the next command.

```
$ date ; pwd ; ls -lt
Fri 14th Nov 15:34
/usr/staff/mac/Cobol
.....
```

Running commands in the background

Some jobs can take a while. Compiling programs, or running programs that sort or update large datafiles can all lock up your terminal for a noticeable amount of time. This can be a good excuse for a coffee break, but if you want to get on with other jobs you can push the slow program into the background. It will then tick over by itself, and leave you free to run other commands. All you need to do is tack an ampersand (**&**) on the end of the command line.

```
$ cob update.cbl -o update &    { compile a program in the background }
$ vi printout.cbl               { while you edit another }
```

The two techniques can be combined, to produce a list of commands with some running in the background – just include the ampersand before the semi-colon.

```
$ update & ; lp printfile ; who
```

In this list, only the 'update' program will be sent to the background.

If you want to run the *whole* list in the background, then enclose the set in brackets and add the ampersand to the end. This list will compile a C program, send its error report to a file, then print the file:

```
$ (cc quicksort.c > errfile ; lp errfile ) &
```

Electronic mail

The majority of Unix users are working alongside others on multi-user systems, and even those running Unix on a PC can work with others through the Internet. As well as sharing resources you can also share ideas and files.

Electronic mail (e-mail) is fashioned along the lines of the traditional postal service, but with added advantages. As with the normal post, e-mail is not delivered to your hand but to your mailbox – so you don't have to be in to receive it. You can look in your mailbox at any point, read messages or not, as you fancy, then put them back into the box or into safe storage elsewhere, or throw them away.

The key advantages claimed for e-mail are that messages are sent almost instantly; copies of a message can be sent to as many people as you like, without retyping; and it's (virtually) free.

e-mail is also easier to ignore than letters and memos! Whether this is an advantage or not depends upon the quality of the correspondence over your system. When people discover e-mail and realise how easy it is to use, there is normally an increase in the quantity of correspondence within the organisation. Some of this will be valuable, much trivial.

There may well be several e-mail programs available on your system, some more sophisticated than others. The simplest, and the one which is certain to be present on any system, is **mail**. You may also find **mailx** or **elm**, or have one as part of a larger office automation package. Though they will differ in their commands and their range of features, all e-mail programs share the same basic features.

When a message is first sent to a user, it will be stored in a temporary mailbox. This is a file, normally located in the '/usr/mail' directory. Any new messages will be added to this file as they arrive, and they will all be kept safe until you choose to deal with them. When you login, on most systems, Unix will check the mail directory and if it finds a file with your name, it will inform you that you have mail. You can access the file at any point during a work session by calling up one or other of the e-mail programs.

mail

This takes the cheap and cheerful approach. It has a limited commands set, but is handy for a quick scan of the mail or for dropping someone a short memo.

Reading the mail

To check your mailbox, type **mail**. If it is empty, you'll be told 'No mail', otherwise the first (oldest) message will be displayed.

```
$ mail
From jill Fri Aug 15 12:38 GMT 1997
Don't forget the team meeting on Monday 18th at 11.30.
Next year's budget top of the agenda.
?
```

The **?** tells you that **mail** is waiting for a command. There are 11, all accessed by typing a single character and [Return].

Command	Effect
[Return] or +	Display next message
p	Redisplay last message
-	Display previous message
d	Delete
s	Save the whole message
s *filename*	Save in the named file
w [*filename*]	As save, but without the message header
m [*user*]	Forward a copy on to the named user
q	Quit
x	Exit – but cancel any deletes
*	Display command summary

Take note

If you save a message, it will be simply added on to the file 'mbox' in your home directory, unless you give a filename.

Sending e-mail

Messages for mailing can be prepared beforehand or typed on-line, while **mail** is running. The on-line method is fine for short messages. Call up **mail** and give the names of the users who are to get copies. Type your message, pressing [Return] at the end of each line. When you have finished, press [Ctrl]-[D].

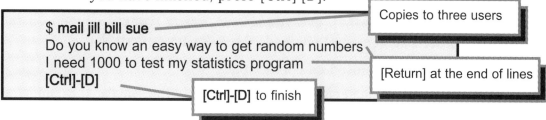

```
$ mail jill bill sue
Do you know an easy way to get random numbers
I need 1000 to test my statistics program
[Ctrl]-[D]
```

Copies to three users

[Return] at the end of lines

[Ctrl]-[D] to finish

As there's no means of editing a line once you have pressed [Return], this approach is not suitable for longer messages.

If you want to write more than a few lines, create your message with **vi** or another text editor, then pass it to mail using I/O redirection. Here, mail takes its input from a text file called 'memo'.

```
$ mail jill bill sue < memo
```

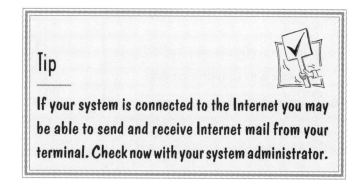

Tip

If your system is connected to the Internet you may be able to send and receive Internet mail from your terminal. Check now with your system administrator.

write – two-way communication

Though mail is transmitted instantly across the system, there's no guarantee that it will be read instantly. If you want immediate feedback, or a two-way conversation, you need a different approach.

write copies text to the terminal of another user. It first sends a note to the recipient, to let them know who is trying to establish a link, e.g. 'Message from dick on tty15'. If the recipient agrees, a two-way link is created. After that, everything one person types is echoed on the other's screen, until one ends the link with a [Ctrl]-[D].

write must be used co-operatively.

- The other user must be open to incoming messages – the command **mesg y** sets you open to receive, while **mesg n** blocks writing.

- The other user must **write** back to you to create the two-way link.

- You must take turns. There is only one screen at either end, and your typing and your correspondent's will become garbled if you both write at the same time. The convention is to write 'o' (over) at the end of a message and 'oo' (over and out) when you finish.

A typical **write** session is shown below. Notice that the sender, Mark, waits for Jill to write to him, before he sends the first message.

Mark's terminal

```
$write jill
Message from jill on tty42
Is Dick over there with you? o
No. Can John help instead? o
Yes. Ask him to come please
oo
```

Jill's terminal

```
Message from mark on tty15
$write mark
Is Dick over there with you? o
No. Can John help instead? o
Yes. Ask him to come please
oo
```

Tip

write can be intrusive. Not everyone appreciates having a message pop up on the screen while they are trying to edit a text file. It won't corrupt the file, but it can break the concentration.

Sharing files

There are essentially two approaches to sharing files – send copies of a file to other users, or arrange for others to have access to a single file. There are several ways to do both – we'll stick to the simplest.

Text files by mail

If you want to send someone a copy of a *text* file, the simplest solution is to use the mail. I/O redirection will let us take the message from a file. If you wanted to give Freda a copy of '*salerep*', you could do this:

```
$ mail freda < salesrep
```

When it gets to the other end, Freda can read it on the mail, or save it to a named file and perhaps print it later. The mail system will have added an information line to the start, but that can be easily removed.

Sharing non-text files

If the file is a compiled program or contains *non-text data*, then the mail method is not feasible. The header line will still be there and the file will be impossible to edit. The answer is to look for a directory that is open to both you and your colleagues. You can copy the file into it, they can copy it out and they will have full ownership of their copy. There may be a common directory open to all of your group. If not, the '/tmp' directory, at the top of the system, is always open to all.

Send a copy to '/tmp' with a line like this:

```
$ cp salesrep /tmp
```

Then other users can get a copy by:

```
$ cp /tmp/salesrep .
```

This line will copy the file into the user's current directory, identified by the dot(.), and will retain its original name. If its destination is elsewhere, then replace the dot with the path. And if the copy is to have a different name, that also should be specified:

```
$ cp /tmp/salesrep accounts/sales.fred
```

Here the copy goes into the 'accounts' sub-directory, and has been renamed to remind the new owner that it came from Fred.

chmod – change permission mode

You may need to do some work before you send out a file for others to copy. The permissions are normally set to allow others to read – and therefore copy – a file. (They can't copy it from your directory because they won't have read access to the directory.) Check the permissions with **ls -l**:

```
$ ls -l salesrep
-rw------- 1 jill  sales  12807  Apr 27 02:15 salesrep
```

The **rw-** shows that you can read and write the file, but the following --- --- shows that no-one else can. (The default permissions may be different on your system.) If you want members of your group, or others to be able to read the file, the second and third set of permissions must have the **r** turned on. We can do this with **chmod**. Its syntax is:

```
$ chmod changes filename
```

The *changes* definition is in three parts:

who: **u** (user/owner)   **g** (group members)   **o** (others) **a** (all)

which way: **+** (add) **-** (remove) **=** (set)

what mode: **r** (read) **w** (write) **x** (execute)

These can be combined freely within the who/which/what format, with settings for different classes of user separated by commas, e.g.

Change	Effect
u+x	Add execute permission for owner (**u**ser)
go-rw	Remove **r**ead and **w**rite for **g**roup and **o**thers
a+r	Add read permission for **g**roup and **o**thers
u=rwx,g=r	Full access for you, **r**ead only for your group

To give all other users read access to your file, you would use:

```
$ chmod a+r salesrep
```

ln – shared access to files

Use this approach when it is important that there is only one copy of the file in the system. This would be the case where the file holds key reference data, such as the account or client database of a business.

You might also use a shared file if you were writing a report and wanted to collect people's comments on it. Their notes could be added directly to the draft file, then incorporated during a final edit.

A shared file can be in a common directory or in a user's directory. Either way, the only person who owns it is the user who created it. Others will have access to it via a *link*. Each will have an entry in their own directory, as if the file were there. It can be copied, moved – and even removed – as if it were a real file. But it's only a link to the file. When you remove a link, you merely close your access to the file.

To set up the shared file, its owner must first set the permissions so that others can read and write to it. Suppose Jill has produced the first draft of the team's report. She opens up the access with:

    $chmod a+rw teamreport   { 'teamreport' is the file }

The others can then make the link with **ln**. They need to give this the full path to the original file and a name for the link. It can have the same name as the original, or a different one. One user might link with this:

    $ ln -s /usr/sales/jill/teamreport teamreport

Another with this, changing the name in the process:

    $ ln -s /usr/sales/jill/teamreport jills_report

ln is usually given with the **-s** option, to make a *symbolic* link (see below).

To try linking, you will need the cooperation of another user.

Possible problems

- You may find that on your system only someone with superuser access can use **ln**. Check with your system administrator.

- The simple **ln** will only create a link between files if they are part of the same overall file structure, within one device. (Where the 'device' is typically a partition on a hard disk.) As all the users' directories are generally on the same device, this shouldn't cause a problem. The alternative **ln -s** sets up a *symbolic link* between files, and this overcomes the barriers between devices. So, if **ln** doesn't work, try **ln -s**.

dc – the desk calculator

dc is an interactive calculator that works in reverse Polish notation. If you have not previously come across this before, it is worth a look just to see how it works. If you are already familiar with it, then here is a calculator that you can use.

The essence of reverse Polish, is that you write the numbers first and the operators afterwards. As numbers are received, they are stored on the *stack*. This is a temporary memory store that runs on the Last In, First Out principle. When an operator is received, **dc** takes the last two numbers off the stack, performs the operation on them and puts the answer back on the stack.

 A calculation string can have any number of terms. Notice this sequence in the example below:

    3 4 5 + *

dc will first store 3, 4 and 5. Meeting '+' it will then take off 4 and 5 – the top two – and add them, putting the result (9) back on the stack. It then reaches '*' and multiplies 9 and 3 to get the answer.

You may need to intermingle operators and numbers to get the right sequence of calculations. Here is what happens as **dc** works through the string 5 4 3 + 2 - *

Input	Action	Stack		
5	Stack it	5		
4	Stack it	4	5	
3	Stack it	3	4	5
+	Add and stack the result	7	5	
2	Stack it	2	7	5
-	Subtract and stack the result	5	5	
*	Multiply and stack the result	25		
p	Print the result	25		

dc recognises a few command letters. The most important ones are:

p   print on screen the number at the top of the stack

c   clear the stack

q   quit

See how **dc** works by trying the sequence show opposite.

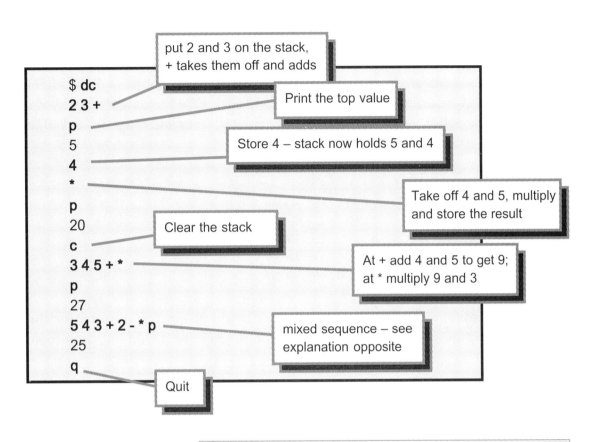

```
$ dc
2 3 +
p
5
4
*
p
20
c
3 4 5 + *
p
27
5 4 3 + 2 - * p
25
q
```

put 2 and 3 on the stack,
+ takes them off and adds

Print the top value

Store 4 – stack now holds 5 and 4

Take off 4 and 5, multiply
and store the result

Clear the stack

At + add 4 and 5 to get 9;
at * multiply 9 and 3

mixed sequence – see
explanation opposite

Quit

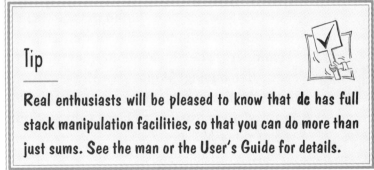

Tip

Real enthusiasts will be pleased to know that **dc** has full
stack manipulation facilities, so that you can do more than
just sums. See the man or the User's Guide for details.

Time and dates

cal – calendar maker

This will give you a calendar for any month or year, from the year dot to way past the point where you will care what the date is. Specify the month alone for a month in the current year, or add the year – in 4-digit format – if necessary.

```
$ cal oct
October
Su Mo Tu We Th Fr  Sa
          1  2  3   4
 5  6  7  8  9  10  11
12 13 14 15 16 17  18
19 20 21 22 23 24  25
26 27 28 29 30 31
```

cal followed by a year number only, will produce a calendar for the whole year, but redirect the output to a file as it won't fit on screen.

```
$ cal 1998 >cal98
```

Now you can print your calendar and save the expense of buying one.

calendar – reminder service

For this to work, you should have a file in your home directory called *calendar*, containing a list of dates and events for which you need reminders. The file layout should follow the pattern given here, with each line having '*Month Day Message*', in that order. The lines do not have to be in date order, and months can be given as full names, abbreviations or by number values – but it must always be month before day.

```
Oct 31 Final Deadline
Nov 4 Proof to copy editor
Nov 11 Page proofs back?
Nov 15 Index & corrected proofs
Nov 21 CRC to printers
Dec 11 Books due in warehouse
```

Just type **calendar** to check on the messages for today and tomorrow – with Friday's tomorrow extending to Monday.

Your system administrator may already be running **calendar** as a service to users, doing a daily check on your file and sending you reminders by mail. If it is not there, write the command into your '*.login*' file, for your own start-of-day reminder service.

sleep – set a delayed action

With **sleep** you can build a timed delay into your system. It could be used in a shell script to hold a screen long enough for it to be read. Use it in a multi-command line, running in the background, to get a timed reminder. The command must be followed by the number of seconds. For example, this line will send a reminder message after 10 minutes:

```
$ (sleep 600 ; echo 'Time to Go') &
```

time – find the duration of a process

Programmers may find this useful for testing the efficiency of alternative routines. A stopwatch is certainly no good for this, as the time a process takes to run depends upon the amount of traffic on the system as well as the complexity of the process.

Type **time** at the start of a command line, and when the process has finished, the system will report on how long it has taken:

```
$ time sort1 <testfile >sorted.out
real 6.5
user 1.3
sys  0.2
```

Three time values will be shown.

real is the total elapsed time,

user is the CPU processing time used by your process

sys is the other active time in the system – for disk-access and the like

Some versions of **time** will also give the user/real fraction as a percentage, to show how much of the elapsed time the CPU spent working on your process. If you are the only active user, this will be close to 100%, but can drop to single figures at busy times.

Summary

❑ Among the many manuals of a Unix system, the most useful is probably the **User Reference**. It is also available on-line through the **man** command.

❑ **Input** is normally from the keyboard and and **output** to the screen, but you can use **redirection** to take data from or send it to files.

❑ The output from one command can be passed to another for further processing, through a **pipe**.

❑ You can give **commands in a list**, for sequential processing, or run them in the **background** while you get on with other jobs.

❑ You can send messages, or files, to other users on your system, through its **mail** facilities.

❑ If the other person agrees, you can **write** interactively on each other's screens.

❑ **Files can be shared** with other users, either by placing them in common directories or by creating multiple links to a shared file.

❑ Before sharing files, you may well have to **change the permissions** so that others can read them.

❑ If you need to do **calculations**, and can cope with reverse Polish notation, use **dc**, the desk calculator.

❑ The **cal** utility will create a calendar. Don't confuse this with **calendar**, which will remind you of appointments.

❑ If you need to set a delay before an event, use **sleep**.

❑ **time** will tell you how long it took the system to work through a process.

5　The shells

Which shell?

When you type a command, you are not talking directly to the Unix operating system, nor does it report back directly to you. Instead, you are working within a **shell** program. This intercepts everything you type, checks to see that it is a meaningful command that it can perform, and either does the job or tells you why it can't. It has other roles as well. It is through the shell that you can control your working environment. The shell also contains its own programming language.

Several different types of shell are found on Unix systems. They are very similar and will all interpret your commands in the same way.

● The **Bourne** shell is standard in Unix System V installations and has the best programming capabilities.

● The **C** shell is also present on most systems. It has a number of features that can make life easier for the user, but has a more limited programming language.

● The **Korn** shell combines the best of both. It is fully compatible with the Bourne shell, so that shell script programs written in either shell will work with the other, and it is as good as the C shell for interactive work.

Check your shell

To find out what type of shell you have, look first at the prompt. If it is a $, you are in a Bourne shell; a % indicates a C shell. If your prompt is neither of these, here's a second way of checking. Type:

```
$ ls -a              { space after the ls }
.    ..    .profile  { or .login and/or .cshrc }
```

If you are working within a Bourne shell, you will have a file called '.profile'. If yours is a C shell, with a **%** prompt, you should see '.login' and '.cshrc' – neither is essential and some systems are set up to run without them. In either case there might also be a '.logout' file.

You are generally better off within the more user-friendly C shell for routine file management and for running applications. When you want to write shell scripts, then the Bourne shell will give you a more comprehensive language and more portable scripts. As the C shell can run Bourne scripts, there's no problem about switching between the two. If you have the Korn shell, then you have the best of both, and can stick to that.

Which one is used as your normal start-up shell depends upon your system administrator, but there is nothing to stop you invoking any other that may be present. To create a new shell use:

sh   for a Bourne shell;
csh for a C shell;
ksh for a Korn shell.

You can have any number of shells, of the same or different types, running simultaneously. Each new one will exist inside, but independently of, the previous one.

Your environment

The '.login', '.profile' and '.cshrc' files are shell programs which run automatically when you log in and set up your working environment. The most important aspect of this is the **PATH**, which determines where Unix should look for programs. Other environmental settings include the style of your prompt, the time zone and the nature of your terminal. The '.logout' file is executed when you logout.

Precisely what is in these files varies enormously. When the system administrator first creates your directory, standard files will be copied into it. You can edit these, to customise the system to your own needs. If you want to see what is in these files, try this:

```
$ cat .profile
...
% cat .login        {or cat .cshrc}
.....
```

Shell scripts

The shell will interpret your instructions one at a time as they are given at the prompt, or work through instructions written into a *script*. This may be a simple sequence of commands, or may be structured loops with and tests, so that commands are repeated or only performed if certain conditions exist (see Chapter 9).

The Bourne shell

If you are not already in a Bourne shell, invoke one now by typing **sh**. This sets up a new one, inside your original shell. There are a number of implications to this, but the most obvious is that when you have finished, you must type **exit** to leave this shell, before you can logout.

If your normal shell is Bourne, have a look now at the '.profile' file. You should see something along the lines of this:

```
$ cat .profile
PATH=/bin:/usr/bin/etc/:$HOME
USER=dick
MAIL=/usr/spool/mail/$USER
export PATH USER MAIL
umask 033
mesg n
```

There may be other things in there as well. In the process of defining your working environment, '.profile' sets variables – principally PATH, USER and MAIL – and runs commands. In the example, it runs **umask** and **mesg**. Let's start with a quick look at what these two.

umask – set file permissions

umask sets the default permissions for any files that you create, albeit in a roundabout way. (At least it looks roundabout from the outside, but no doubt makes programming simpler at system level.) It works by *masking* – filtering out what is not wanted – rather than by defining what is wanted. To understand it, we need to go back to **chmod**. Last time we looked at this (page 66) we changed permissions like this:

```
$ chmod g+wx common.prog
```

If you had to set all the permissions for a file, the argument string could become somewhat ungainly:

```
$ chmod u+rwx,g=rx,o-rwx newfile
$ ls -l newfile
-rwxr-x— 1 fiona staff          2407 Nov 10 09:48 newfile
```

Permissions can be set more compactly by using numbers to represent the codes. '**r**' is worth 4, '**w**' 2 and '**x**' 1. Add them together to get the permissions for each category of user.

Done with numbers, the equivalent of that last command would be:

$ **chmod 750 newfile**

Similarly, 744 would give you full access, but restrict your group and others to read only. Now we can go back to **umask**.

umask sets the number to be taken from 777 to define the permissions.

base	777		
umask	033		
result	744	giving	rwxr—r—

mesg – permit write messages

This controls whether or not your terminal is open for others to **write** to (page XX). As unwanted messages can be disruptive, it is a sensible precaution to include **mesg n** in the *.profile*. When you want to communicate with others via your terminal, open the lines with:

$ **mesg y**

Special characters

Take care typing these characters in a command line or script – they have special meanings for the shell:

* ? [ ] | ; : { } ( ) < > << >> $ = ' "

Sometimes you will want to use the characters for themselves, or pass them through the shell and on to a command without being interpreted. In that case, the character must be 'escaped' by preceding it with a backslash. (\). For example, try this:

$ **echo ***

(**echo** displays whatever follows – text or the values of variables.)

You should find that it lists the files in your current directory. The '**'* wildcard has been expanded into all the filenames. Now try:

$ **echo ***

This time it should simply print the asterisk. The backslash has removed its special meaning.

Variables

Like any other programming language, the shell supports the use of **variables** – named places in memory in which data can be stored. Unlike other languages, in the shell, all variables are of the same sort – simple text. Numbers can be stored in them, but only as text. If you want to calculate with variables, special techniques are needed.

To assign a value to a variable, use an expression of the type:

    variable=value

e.g.

    $ name=Fred

Do not put spaces around the '='. If you do, the shell will try to treat 'name' as a command and give you a 'Not Found' message. If the value consists of more than a single word, it must be enclosed in quotes:

    $ name= 'Dick Turpin'

When you want to get the value back out of the variable, its name must be preceded by the dollar sign ($).

    $echo $name
    Dick Turpin
    $

Try it again without the dollar sign. What do you get?

To see how the shell handles numbers, set up two variables, giving them number values, and try to add them. Your screen display should be something like this:

```
$ num1=42
$ num2=99
$ echo $num1 + $num2
42 + 99
```

As you can see, the shell does not recognise numbers as values, but as strings of text digits. It is possible to force it to evaluate a variable, and we will come back to that in Chapter 9 where we look more closely at shell programming. Often, however, there's not much point. If you wanted a calculating program, there are better languages than the shell. It is designed for manipulating commands and text files.

Exporting variables

A variable normally exists only in the shell in which it was created. If you want to make its values accessible to other shells, you must force this with the **export** command.

Test it with this sequence:

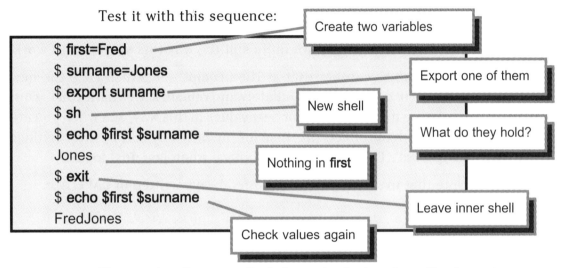

```
$ first=Fred
$ surname=Jones
$ export surname
$ sh
$ echo $first $surname
Jones
$ exit
$ echo $first $surname
FredJones
```

Create two variables

Export one of them

New shell

What do they hold?

Nothing in **first**

Leave inner shell

Check values again

This might all seem a little hypothetical – after all, why enter a new shell if you are going to lose your variables – but it is important. It matters because when you run a shell script with **sh**, it creates a new shell to run the script. So, if you have variables, created at the prompt or in a script, and you want to access them from within another script, they must be exported.

Environment variables

Environment variables, or **shell parameters**, are built into the shell, and store information about your working environment. Some will have already been set for you; some cannot, or should not, be changed. Others are a matter of personal choice and can be reset to adjust your working environment. Look carefully at these, for the standard settings may not quite suit the way that you want to work.

The variables can be reset at the prompt – in which case the new setting will take effect immediately and remain active until you log out or change it again. Test your new values in this way, and when you are happy with the effects, fix them for the future by editing their settings in '.profile'. They will then be in place when you next login.

Note that the shell parameters are always written in CAPITALS.

HOME

This stores the path to your home directory and should not be changed. Echo it to the screen to see where you are:

```
$ echo $HOME    { don't forget the $ }
/usr/staff/mac
```

PATH

When you type in the name of a program, or give a command (and a command is simply a program provided by the system) how does Unix know where to find the program? It could be in any of your directories, up in the main '/bin' or anywhere else to which you have access.

There's a second, related problem. A typical Unix system will have hundreds of commands and utilities available to its users. If you are writing your own programs, there's a fair chance that at some time or another you will write one with the same name as an existing one. How will Unix know whether you want your 'sort' program or the 'sort' that it's got tucked away in the bin?

The path tells the system where to look for programs, and – just as importantly – where to look first. It consists of a sequence of directory names, in search order, and should include all the open-access system directories plus those of yours that contain programs. A standard path should have been defined for you in '.profile'.

To find the current setting of the PATH variable, type this:

$ echo $PATH

If the standard setting is not the most suitable for the way you want to work, redefine it.

Path definition

Paths are defined in the same way as other variables. Separate the directory names by colons, with no spaces between them. e.g.

$ PATH=/bin:/bin/usr:.

Given this path, when you type a command, the system will look first in '/bin', then in '/usr/bin' and finally in your current directory (dot). It stops looking as soon as it finds a program with a matching name.

The order and choice of directories to include in your path depends upon the location of program files and the type of user that you are. As the search for a match proceeds in path order, you will get a faster response from those at the start of the path. So, find out the location of the programs that you use most frequently and place their directories at the start. For most people, this will mean that the path should begins with '/bin:/usr/bin ..' which is where you will find **ls, rm** and similar file management commands. This is how the default paths begin on most systems.

For **business users**, who are mainly running word-processing, accounts packages or other application software, the path should start with those applications' directories.

Programmers will probably want their current directory – identified by the single dot (.) – early in the path. If you intend to write your own utility programs, store these in your main directory or a special sub-directory and write its name early in the path. The variable **$HOME** stores the route to your directory – use that in your path instead of typing the full route. e.g.

$ PATH=.:$HOME:$HOME/utils:/bin:/usr/bin

This puts your current directory, your main directory and your sub-directory 'utils' at the head of the search path.

PS1 and PS2

Like a personalised prompt, rather than that boring '$' that everybody has? These parameters define the prompts. **PS1** is the normal prompt ($), **PS2** the one that you will see sometimes when you give an incomplete command line (>).

You could give yourself more interesting prompts with something along the lines of:

```
$ PS1='Next job:'
$ PS2='And the rest of it ..'
```

There's no real limit to the length of the prompt string, except the practical one. I've known people with prompts that read 'What is your command, Oh great master of the Unixverse:' – or words to that effect. It may massage your ego, but it doesn't leave much space across the screen for the commands!

The default prompt parameters are set by the shell, but your system manager may have set up alternatives in your *.profile*.

MAIL

If this is set, the shell will check your mailbox when you login and inform you if there is anything in it.

The definition identifies the file in which the system stores your incoming mail. This will be labelled with your user name and will be held in the mail directory. It should look something like this:

```
MAIL=/usr/spool/mail/fred
```

You should find a line of this type in your '.profile' (if you have one), though on some systems it can be set at a deeper level. Echo MAIL to the screen to view your setting.

? – exit status

When a command or program has ended, it returns a value to the shell, where it is held in the parameter '?'. This value will be either 0, to signify True, or 1, signifying False, depending upon what happened within the command. Though interesting, this is irrelevant unless you specifically want to know the outcome of a command, or want an action to be conditional upon that outcome.

Detour – using the exit status

cmp – file comparison

cmp will show the use of the exit status. This compares two files and either reports any differences or returns an exit status. Its syntax is:

cmp [-ls] *file1 file2*

The **-s** option suppresses the display of differing lines. Use it if you just want to know if two files are the same – miss it out to see the details. Try it with files that you know are the same – then again with two that are different – and test the exit status after each comparison.

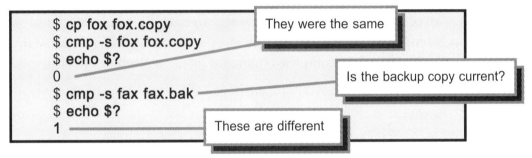

```
$ cp fox fox.copy                    They were the same
$ cmp -s fox fox.copy
$ echo $?
0                                    Is the backup copy current?
$ cmp -s fax fax.bak
$ echo $?
1                   These are different
```

Having established that the backup copy is not up to date, you might now create a new backup. We can automate this, and get the system to check and act on the exit status.

Conditional command lines

A command line may contain two distinct commands, with the execution of the second being conditional upon the result of the first. There are two possible conditional links:

&&   Do if true (exit status = 0)
|| Do if false (exit status = 1)

A line which created a new backup if the old one was no longer valid would look like this:

$ **cmp -s fox fox.bak || cp fox fox.bak**

Similarly, a line to remove an unwanted copy would take this form:

$ **cmp -s fox hound && rm hound**

Conditional commands can be very powerful when used in shell scripts, allowing you to process a whole directory in a few lines.

The C shell

The C shell was developed at the University of California at Berkeley as a more user-friendly alternative to the Bourne shell. Its basic function of command line interpretation is identical, and its predefined shell variables overlap with those of Bourne. But there are two features which really mark it out from the Bourne shell, and which make life in the C shell significantly easier. These are the existence of **aliases** and the **history** facility.

Aliases

An alias is an alternative name for something, and one used in preference to the real name. Unix aliases can make the system easier to use by reducing complex command lines to simpler short forms.

To list the aliases, if any, that have been set for you, type the command:

% **alias**

An alias can be given in a command line – in which case it is active for that session only – or written into the *.cshrc*. As the system runs through the commands in this file at the start of every session, your aliases will then be always there for you. The line takes the form:

% **alias** *new_name command_string*

For instance, to set an alias so that you could use a DOS-style 'dir' rather than 'ls', you would want the line:

% **alias dir ls**

Try it now. Type it in at the prompt, then type **dir** to test it.

The *command_string* can also include optional arguments. In this case, enclose the string in single quotes. This will give you a simple way to get a fully-detailed directory listing:

% **alias ll 'ls -la'**

Think about the way you use the system. Are there lengthy command lines that you have to type in regularly? An alias to simplify changing into a frequently-used directory might be handy. If you had a sub-directory called *textfiles*, changing into it from elsewhere in your area would normally involve getting back to your home directory, then changing down from there – or giving a fuller path. This alias would reduce it to a few keystrokes:

% **alias text 'cd $HOME/textfiles'**

File specifications and aliases

When you type a command line that includes a simple alias like the ones above, Unix expands the alias but leaves the rest of the line untouched. Any file specifications are therefore carried across. Thus:

% **ll *.txt**

expands to:

% **ls -la *.txt**

This gives a detailed listing of your text files, as desired.

The situation is a little more complicated if the original command line includes a pipeline to another program. Here the file specification will be embedded in the command. The solution lies in the combination of symbols '\!*'. This typically compact and forbidding phrase translates to mean 'pick up whatever follows the alias'. (Why it works should be clearer after you have read the section 'Editing command lines' on page 89.) For instance, if you wanted a full directory listing, run through a screenful at a time via **pg**, the command line would be:

% **ls -l *filespec* | pg**

Create an 'lpg' (long, paged) alias with:

% **alias lpg 'ls -l \!* |pg'**

Typing **lpg *.pas** would then be equivalent to **ls -l *.pas |pg**.

Explore the possibilities of aliases, and when you have found some that look as though they may be really useful, edit you ' .cshrc' file – create a new one if there isn't one there already – and write the alias lines into it. Next time you login, Unix will work through the '.cshrc' and set up the aliases.

History

The history facility keeps a record of your most recent commands. This gives you a way of finding what it was that you did that produced any particular good – or bad – results. It also makes for more efficient working, especially if you are an indifferent typist. As past commands are stored, they can be recalled and reused – and they can be edited, to correct errors or to vary their effect. The longer the command line, the more you will appreciate these repeat and edit facilities.

You should find that history has been set up for you already. Try it:

```
% history
13 cd
16 ls
17 alias dir ls
....
23 vi .cshrc
24 history
```

If it is present you will see a list of the last dozen or so commands, numbered in the order that they were given. If you want to see those that are further back in the record, give the number of the first and last that you want. (Or rather, take a guess as you are unlikely to know their numbers.) For example:

```
% history 5 20
 5 pwd
...
...
18 ls -C *.pas
19 alias ll ls -la
20 ll textfiles
```

If the history facility has not been turned on, set it up now by the line:

```
% set history=20
```

This will store the last 20 commands. Now type **date**, **ls**, **pwd** and a few other commands, to put something in the file.

With **history** active, you can recall any command in the file by typing an exclamation mark followed by either the command number (counting from login), or the start of the command string. Let's take some examples based on the first history given above. Using the 'start of command string' approach:

```
% !v
vi .cshrc
```

The system has scanned back through the file and picked up the last command starting with a 'v'.

If there were several starting with the same letter, and you wanted an earlier one, you would have to type enough letters to distinguish it. So, to get **ls -C *.pas** (number 18), and not the later **ll textfiles**, you would type:

```
% !ls
```

There's a quickie variation on this. A double exclamation mark will repeat the last command, whatever it was.

Adding to recalled command lines

As with aliases, these abbreviations are expanded by the shell into the full commands before being sent off for processing. As a result, you can add parameters or pipes to the !recall and these will be incorporated into the command.

Suppose you have just done 'ls -la' and discovered that the directory is so full that most of it has scrolled off the screen. You should have piped it through 'pg' to get a controlled display. This will do it:

```
% !! |pg
```

If **ls -la** was the last job, the shell will expand the recall into **ls -la |pg**.

This quick repeat facility is of most use to those who regularly perform a limited set of commands. This is often true for programmers. Their normal flow of work is to edit a source file, attempt to compile it, edit again to correct errors, compile it again, and so on until it works. Then a test run will be incorporated into the sequence, to give an edit-compile-test cycle.

A typical history might read:

```
10 vi myfile.c
11 cc myfile.c -o myfile
12 vi myfile.c
13 cc myfile.c -o myfile
14 vi myfile.c
15 cc myfile.c -o myfile
16 myfile
17 vi myfile.c
18 cc myfile.c -o myfile
19 myfile
```

With a history, the command sequence can be reduced to **!v!, !c, !m** – which must save time and typing errors.

The **command number** method works in the same way, except that you type in the number from the history file, rather than the initial characters. With that last history, you could get **vi myfile.c**, the 17th command by:

    % !17

The numbering can also be done on a relative basis, counting back from the current command. Thus:

    % !-3

would also give the 17th command, **vi myfile.c**, assuming that your current one is number 20.

These approaches are of limited value as it takes generally more effort to recall the history file and scan for the number, or work out how far back you gave a command, than it does to type it out afresh. It only makes sense if you want to repeat a particularly long and complex line – especially if it differs only slightly from another previous line. In that case the 'start of command' approach would not work efficiently.

Editing command lines

Someone took a lot of time and trouble to build a number of clever, but not very user-friendly, editing facilities into the C shell. Two are worth learning – how to substitute characters to correct minor errors, and how to slice words out of a line. If you are interested in what else is available, you can look them up in the Manual entry for **csh**.

Substitution

You can change the characters in the previous command line by writing the caret (^) followed by the characters to be removed, then a second carat and the new characters. For example:

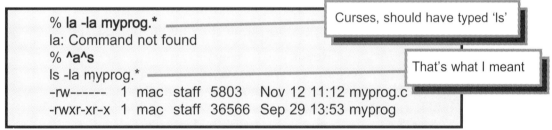

```
% la -la myprog.*                      Curses, should have typed 'ls'
la: Command not found
% ^a^s
ls -la myprog.*                        That's what I meant
-rw------   1 mac  staff  5803    Nov 12 11:12 myprog.c
-rwxr-xr-x  1 mac  staff  36566   Sep 29 13:53 myprog
```

This form of substitution only works on the *previous* line. But don't forget the history list – you can get at older commands by !recalling them. If you do not want to execute the recalled command, add **:p** to the end of the recall instruction. The line is then **p**rinted, but not run.

Suppose that you had recently copied a file from a distant directory into another subdirectory, with the line:

> % **cp ../groupwork/reports/sales/mayjuly92.txt accounts**

After working on it, you then want to copy the next quarter's report from that same place into your 'accounts' directory. A simple !recall would bring the line back, but also copy the file again, overwriting your work. Writing **:p** immediately after the !recall – no space – will make it print only. The editing sequence then runs like this:

```
                                       Recall the copy line, without execution
% !cp:p
% cp ../groupwork/reports/sales/mayjuly92.txt accounts
% ^mayjuly^augoct                      Make your changes
cp ../groupwork/reports/sales/augoct92.txt accounts
```

Slicing

Each word in a command line can be referred to by number– a word is something with spaces on either side. This allows you to copy part of a previous command into the current line. Words are specified by writing : (colon) and the number or one of the characters ^ $ *.

:0	first word (the command)
:n	the *n*th word
:n1-n2	the set from word n1 to word n2
:^	second word (first argument or parameter)
:$	last word
:*	all the words following the command

Let's take some examples based on the line: **ls -ls *.txt | pg**

Code	Result	
:0	ls	first word (command)
:^ or :1	-la	second word (first argument)
:0-2	ls -la *.tx	words 0 to 2
:$ or :3	|pg	fourth and last word
:*	-la |pg	all the words after 'ls'

To use these in practice, we also have to specify the line that we are cutting from. Let's carry on from that long command line we had earlier. Having copied the file into the 'accounts' directory, we now want to move into it to work there.

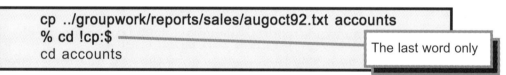

```
cp ../groupwork/reports/sales/augoct92.txt accounts
% cd !cp:$
cd accounts
```
The last word only

Notice that the word designator follows immediately after the !recall.

!cp :$ (with a space) would not work.

Words can be sliced out of the **current line** in the same way. This may sound slightly pointless but cast your mind back to the aliases. There you met the expression '\!*'. The single exclamation mark refers to the current line, and the asterisk to all the words that follow the command. (The backslash in front of the exclamation mark stops the shell from expanding it within the **alias** line.)

C shell variables

Some of the predefined variables in the C shell are directly equivalent to the shell parameters of Bourne; others are specific to the C shell. Here is a small selection of the most useful variables to know.

setenv and set

Use **setenv** to assign values to environment variables, or **set** to other variables, in the form:

> % **set prompt='What now?'**

A simple **set** will display the current values held by the shell variables.

home – login directory

This is equivalent to **HOME**, and contains the name of your home directory. It is set by the system at login, and shouldn't be changed.

The tilde (~) is a handy short form for **$HOME** (which gives the path to your home directory). This line would copy a file from '/tmp' to your 'letters' directory, wherever you were in the system at the time.

> % **cp /tmp/oct1992.txt ~/letters**

mail – path to the mailbox (environment variable)

This is equivalent to Bourne's **MAIL**. It holds the path to your mailbox. Echo it to the screen and you should see something like:

> **mail=/usr/spool/mail/fred**

path – directories to search (environment variable)

This is identical to the Bourne PATH.

prompt - input prompt string

The C shell has only the one prompt and the default is **%**. It can usefully be redefined. Try this – with your own name:

> % **set prompt = 'mac[\!]->'**
> mac[25]->

The '!' in the prompt expands into the current job number, permitting a more effective use of the history list. When you are giving a command that you know you may well want to use later, make a note of its number. You can then recall it by number when you want it.

Summary

❏ The **shell** is a program which interprets your commands and controls your working environment.

❏ There may be **more than one type of shell** available on your Unix system – the Bourne and C shells are both widely used.

❏ If your normal shell is **Bourne**, you should have a **.profile** in your home directory. This holds the parameters and commands that control your working environment.

❏ Use **umask** to set the default permissions for new files.

❏ Data can be stored in **variables** in the shell.

❏ Environment variables, also called **shell parameters**, include **HOME**, which holds the path to your home directory, and **PATH**, which tells the system where to look for programs.

❏ The **exit status** tells you whether or not a command has been performed successfully.

❏ The **C shell** is more user-friendly than Bourne. Amongst other things, it allows you to set up **aliases** that can simplify regularly-used commands.

❏ The **history** keeps a record of the most recent commands. They can be recalled from this list by number, or by giving their initial letters.

❏ You can recall, **edit and reuse command lines**, in the C shell.

❏ The **C shell variables** serve much the same purposes as the Bourne shell parameters.

6 Working with files

Directory management

On a multi-user system, the routine backing up is usually done for you, so keeping files safe is not the chore that it can be on a PC – but keeping them organised can be more difficult. The problem is that you have apparently unlimited disk space. It's not unlimited, of course, and the system administrator may well complain if you spread yourself too freely. But nothing tells you how little space is left. **ls** doesn't, and even **du** only tells you how much you have used, not how much remains. As a result, most of us tend to leave files around, clogging up our directories, long after they have ceased to be of use.

Good directory management is mainly a matter of structure and working habits, rather than of using any special commands. You should by now have created directories for each area of your work. If they contain so many files that a full listing more than fills the screen, now is the time to trim and to sub-divide. First, remove files that really are of no further use, and any compiled programs that are not immediately wanted – retaining the source code so that they can be recompiled later. Compiled programs tend to be large – a typical 20Kb Cobol text file, for example, compiles into a 300+Kb program.

Is it junk?

If a straight **rm** is too final for you, make deletion a two-stage process. Set up a new directory called 'junk' (or something similar). Then instead of removing a file, move it to this directory, from which it can be reclaimed if wanted. At the end of every week or so, check your 'junk', and clear out those files that are clearly surplus. If you work in a C shell, you can create an alias to manage the move/remove efficiently.

```
% alias junkit 'rm $1 ~/junk'
```

For long-term storage, create a new sub-directory, perhaps called 'old', and move into it those that are no longer in regular use but may be wanted later. Each directory should have its own 'old', so that files can be moved easily in and out of cold storage.

If there are still too many active files in the same place, look for ways that you could sub-divide them. It's best to make the new directory at the same level as the split one, rather than a sub-directory of it.

For example, a computing student might have this directory structure.

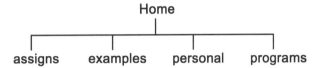

The 'programs' directory has grown to the point where something must be done. Some programs are in C, but most are in Pascal and these fall into two main groups – mathematical and file-handling. Once a program is finished, it is not normally needed again, but can be useful for reference. These could be stashed into a sub-directory.

Here is a possible reorganisations of the structure. 'programs' has disappeared and been replaced by 'filepas', 'mathpas', 'otherpas' and 'C'. Each of these has a single sub-directory called 'old'. No file is more than two levels down, so that, working from the home directory, the longest pathname that ever has to be used is 'otherpas/old'.

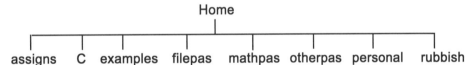

Here's how the directory structure would be if our student took the sub-sub-sub- approach. 'programs' has been divided into 'Pascal' and 'C'. 'Pascal' is then divided into 'maths', 'files' and 'others'. There will now by paths such as 'programs/Pascal/other/old'. Try typing that in a hurry, and you will see why it's best to have as few levels as possible.

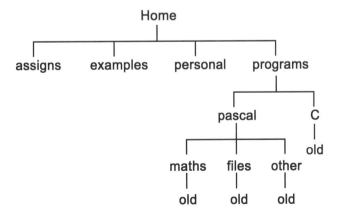

find – locate a file

It is alarmingly easy to lose track of files, unless you are highly organised in your directory structures and choice of filenames. Even the best Unix users have bad days when they cannot remember a filename or its directory, and at times like that, any help in locating files is welcome. Fortunately Unix comes equipped with a number of utilities that can tackle the problem from several directions.

find offers a very sophisticated search facility, and is ideal if you know the name of a file, but not its location. This is one of the more powerful commands, and in Unix power and simplicity rarely go together. **find** locates files that match given criteria, and may then go on to perform actions if matching files are present. The search criteria can be name, size, type or time since last accessed – amongst others – and the search runs through all the sub-directories below the start point. Combine it with **rm** or **cp** and you have a neat file management utility.

The basic shape of the command is:

find *start_of_path options_and_arguments action*

start_of_path specifies the point at which the search begins. Start somewhere above the directory in which you believe the file to be. If you haven't got a clue, first use **cd** to go to your home directory . The *start_of_path* can then be a dot (.) meaning 'the current directory'.

Not all options take arguments, and several options may well be used at once. Actions are also optional.

-print

-print will make **find** print the names of those that match – if you do not use it, you won't see what it finds! The names will be given with their full paths – and hence their locations. If you want a permanent copy of the output for later reference, >redirect it into a file, or add a **tee** pipe fitting to get both immediate screen output and a file.

-name

-name *filename* is the key to finding files. The option is followed by a filename or wildcard expression. Give the filename in full if you know it and want only that file.

96

For example, to find the file 'urgent.memo' that you wrote last week and forgot to mail:

```
$ cd                        { go to home directory }
$ find . -name urgent.memo -print
/usr/staff/tony/jobs/urgent.memo
```

There it is, in the 'jobs' directory. If Tony had got the name wrong, so that it could not be found, **find** would have given no feedback – not even a 'Not found' message.

If you are unsure of the name, or want to find a set of related files, use wildcard expressions. These must be enclosed in quotes so that the expression is passed through the shell to **find**, before it is expanded. Suppose that Tony was looking for the minutes of a meeting held in July, and could remember only that the name would have started with *jul...* or *july...* He might have tried this:

```
$ find . -name 'jul*' -print
/usr/staff/tony/sales/jul15.rpt
/usr/staff/tony/sales/jul25.memo
/usr/staff/tony/accounts/jul7invs.sum
/usr/staff/tony/misc/jul30dti.mins
/usr/staff/tony/personal/julie.invite
```

The **find** has turned up a promising file in the 'misc' directory. That will be worth closer inspection. It has also turned up an invitation from Julie, which Tony may also have forgotten about!

```
$ find . -name '*.pas' -print |tee pasfiles
```

This time the command will produce a list of all the Pascal source files. The |**tee** pipeline splits the output, giving a screen display and storing a permanent record of the list in 'pasfiles'.

Using an alias

The **find -name** is so handy that it is worth creating an alias (in a C or Korn shell) to make it easier to use. A suitable alias would be:

```
alias fnd find . -name '\!*' -print
```

The '**\!***' expression carries your file specification through to the full command line. To use it, you would go to a suitable point on the directory tree – it runs from the current directory – and give the command in the form:

fnd *filename*.

-type finds files of a given type, with the types specified by the letters:

b	block special	**c**	character special
d	directory	**p**	pipe
f	plain file		

You can probably forget about 'block' and 'character' files – these are external devices – and the 'pipe' files are for advanced users. However, the other two are immediately useful.

Give **find** with the 'd' option to see your directory structure. Here's what I got, running it from my home directory:

```
$ find . -type d -print
/usr/staff/mac
/usr/staff/mac/basic
/usr/staff/mac/pascal
/usr/staff/mac/.iosmail
/usr/staff/mac/progassigns
/usr/staff/mac/qmassigns
/usr/staff/mac/c
/usr/staff/mac/Mail
/usr/staff/mac/example
/usr/staff/mac/micropro
```

Time options

-atime **-ctime** are very similar options, and will match any files that were last accessed (**-atime**) or changed (**-ctime**) on a given day. The day is specified by number, counting back from today, with today being 0.

The **-ctime** option is probably used more than the other. A typical use for it is to find those files that have been changed during the day and that therefore should be copied to the backup tape overnight. The command line to find today's files would be:

```
$find . -ctime 0 -print
```

-exec *command* passes each located file across to the following *command*. This is given in its normal form, except that a pair of empty curly brackets {} replace the file argument and the command must be ended by an escaped semi-colon \;. For example, to remove all the *.bak* files – from all your directories – run this from your home directory:

$ find . -name '*.bak' -exec rm {} \;

It's not always plain sailing. You might expect this line to copy those files that have been changed today into a directory called 'backup'.

$ find . -ctime 0 -exec cp {} backup \;

This will do more than you bargained for! As the current directory and any sub-directories are also files to Unix, and as they are updated when any of their files are changed, **find** also matches those. As a result, all their files are copied across to 'backup' as well! There is a solution to this, but it is takes a shell script, not just a tweak to the command line. In case you are interested, here's one way to tackle it.

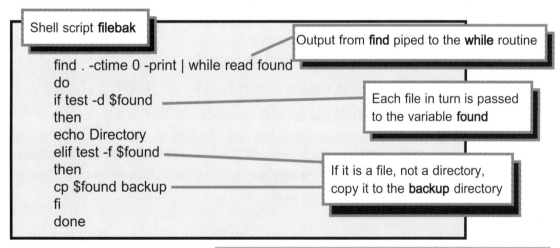

Shell script **filebak**

Output from **find** piped to the **while** routine

```
find . -ctime 0 -print | while read found
do
if test -d $found
then
echo Directory
elif test -f $found
then
cp $found backup
fi
done
```

Each file in turn is passed to the variable **found**

If it is a file, not a directory, copy it to the **backup** directory

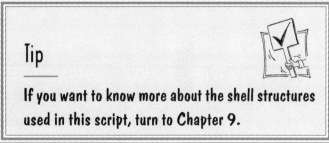

Tip

If you want to know more about the shell structures used in this script, turn to Chapter 9.

Compound expressions

find can test two or more criteria at once. You might, for instance, want to track down the text files created in the last week, or to try two alternative names for a file.

If the link between the tests is an AND, i.e. both tests must be true for the criteria to be met, then write the two tests in a pair of ( ) curved brackets. Care needed here! Brackets have a meaning to the shell, so to pass them through to find, they must be escaped by \backslash.

```
$ find . \( -name *.txt -ctime 7 \) -print
```

This will find all those files with a .txt extension, created or edited in the last week.

Where the link between the criteria is OR, i.e. either one or both can be true, you must use the operator **-o.** Suppose you were looking for a file which you called either *annual.rpt* or *end_of_year.doc*. Rather than do two separate searches, you can join the alternative tests with **-o**, enclosed in brackets. The **find** command is then:

```
$ find . \( -name annual.rpt -o -name end_of_year.doc \) -print
/usr/staff/bill/text/old/annual.rpt
/usr/staff/bill/text/backup/end_of_year.doc
```

Note that the **-name** option is specified for each test.

In this example, **find** has turned up copies of the file under each of the names. This is not an unusual experience. A back-up copy made towards the end of a long session is easy to forget, and programmers often generate many files holding variations of the same program, as they refine their original draft.

Tip

This is not specific to **find**, but applies in any situation where you want to pass an AND/OR expression through the shell to a command.

---

grep – search text files

grep – the 'general regular expression pattern matcher' – searches through files and displays any lines that contain a given string. Its primary purpose is to search database files – i.e. those where each line contains one record, subdivided into fields (see page 130). You give it a value to be looked for, and it will produce a set of records that contain a matching string. But its also provides a quick way of locating text within any text file. If the displayed line has all the data you need, then no further action is needed, and if not, at least you know where to start looking when you load the file into **vi** or whatever editor. Finally you can use it to find files where you have forgotten the filenames but can remember a key word or phrase.

At its simplest, **grep** takes the form:

> grep *expression filename*

The *expression* can be a simple string – either a single word or a phrase enclosed in quotes – or may contain special characters that influence the nature of the search.

Searching within files

Let's start with simple strings. For example, you want to send some mail to Fiona, but do not know her user name. That information is contained in the '/etc/passwd' file. All users have read access to this – the actual passwords are either written there in an encoded version, or stored elsewhere, depending upon the system. You can't write to the file, delete it or change it in any way – only the superuser has that kind of access to '/etc/passwd' – but read access is all you need for **grep**. This command will scan the file and display the line containing 'Fiona':

> $ grep Fiona /etc/passwd
> fp295:*:295:102:Fiona Pearce,admin:/u/staff/admin/fiona:/bin/sh

This tells us that her user name is 'fp295' – it is fairly common practice to create user names from initials and user numbers. At the far right of the line you can see her home directory and login shell. This system uses the Bourne shell, activated by **/bin/sh** at login.

Searching for files

If you replace the filename with a wildcard expression, you can search through a set of files. This is how you can find files when you have forgotten their names, but can remember something of what they contained. All you need is a key string that will pick up the right file.

The management have just replied to your memo about car parking. They want to discuss your ideas in depth, so you had best dig out your file copy. But what was it called? You haven't a clue, but can clearly recall using the phrase 'laudably democratic'. It's not an expression you often use and should be an excellent key. The grep line then runs:

```
$ grep 'laudably democratic ' *
meters: be laudably democratic to allocate a slot to your secretary
```

Now you remember that you called the file 'meters' as you had been forced to park on those for the previous week.

Programmers find **grep** useful for tracking down routines in existing programs, either to copy them into a new program or to check on their usage. I'm struggling with the 'strcmp' function in a new C program, and the **man** entry is little help. Where and how have I used it successfully in the past?

```
$ grep strcmp *.c
lockup.c:       if (strcmp(outfile, "temp.$$$") == 0)
treedir.c:          case 1:  if (strcmp(n,branch->name) < 0)
treedir.c:          case 2:  if (strcmp(e,branch->date) < 0)
```

That finds examples in two programs. One of these should give me the help I need.

grep options

-i With this set, **grep ignores** the distinction between capitals and lower case. For example, to find Simon's user name, I could use this:

```
$ grep -i simon /etc/passwd
eagle:*:236:499:Simon  Row,NDCS1:/u/student/dip1/eagle:/bin/csh
kiwi:*:240:499:simon  brown,NDCS1:/u/student/dip1/kiwi:/bin/csh
wasp:*:350:108:SIMON  GREEN,FCIT:/u/student/fcit/wasp:/bin/csh
```

(This system has an idiosyncratic approach to user names.)

The key word for **grep** could equally well have been 'SIMON', or 'Simon'. The result would have been the same.

-c Will **count** lines. With this option set, **grep** suppresses the display of lines and tells you only how many contained matching strings. You can use it to find how many records in a database hold a particular value. For example, how many First Year Diploma students do we have? They are identified by 'dip1' in their '/etc/passwd' entries.

```
$ grep -c dip1 /etc/passwd
38
```

The answer is a simple number. If the search extends across more than one file, then each filename is listed, with a count value at the end. In which C programs can I find examples of the 'strcat' function?

```
$ grep -c strcat *.c
bsearch.c:0
cclean.c:0
...
test.c:0
tidyup.c:4
tree.c:0
treedir.c:4
wpr.c:3
```

tidyup.c, *tree.c* and *wpr.c* all contain several examples of its use.

-l This option suppresses the display of **lines** containing the matched expression. At the simplest, you can use it where you are only interested in the matching files, and not in the details of the containing lines – in which Pascal programs, for example, have I used 'REWRITE'?

```
$ grep -l REWRITE *.pas
linker.pas
print.pas
stocktest.pas
upd.pas
update.pas
```

At a more advanced level, you can use **grep** expressions to get filenames, which are then passed on to commands through a pipe.

-n Asks **grep** to show line **numbers.** I suspect that this option is mainly intended for use with **ed**, the old line-based text editor, but it still has some value. As it will give you the line as well as the file, it pinpoints the location of items and can speed up later editing.

```
$ grep -n strcmp *.c
lockup.c:84:     if (strcmp(outfile, "temp.$$$") == 0)
treedir.c:39:     case 1:  if (strcmp(n,branch->name) < 0)
treedir.c:40:     case 2:  if (strcmp(e,branch->date) < 0)
```

-f *filename* Takes the expression from a file. This is handy if you are using the same complex expression frequently. Write it into a file, then give the filename instead of the search string.

Suppose, for example, that you were afflicted by the unfortunate habit of writing 'at this moment in time' when you really mean 'now'. It is something that you do unconsciously, so you have to check your texts from time to time to remove it. Try this. Create a file called 'now', consisting of the line:

'at this moment in time'   { including the quotes }

You can then scan your text files for this clumsy Americanism by the command:

```
$ grep -f now *.txt
```

-v   Reverses the match. The effect is to output every line in the specified files except those that match the pattern. Use with care. You could get more than you anticipated!

grep search patterns

grep has a set of special characters that can be used to construct patterns containing wildcards, instead of a simple string. They can also specify whereabouts in the lines to search for a match.

The main **grep** wildcard is . (dot), which stands for any single character.

$ grep 'Sm.th' /etc/passwd

This would find any occurrence of 'Smith', 'Smyth', 'Smythe', 'Smithers', 'Smithson', 'McSmith' or similar. All that matters is that the word contains 'Sm' and is followed after a gap of one character by 'th'. The characters before and after are irrelevant as **grep** finds partial and whole word matches.

The asterisk (*) – the normal shell wildcard – serves a different purpose here. In **grep** it is a repeater. Write this after a character to match any number of repetitions of that character. Its most common use is after dot, so that the pair act like the normal shell wildcard.

$ grep 'John R.*son' namelist

This will find 'John Robertson', 'John Robinson', 'John Robson' or any other John whose surname starts with 'R' and ends with 'son'.

Alternative characters, or a range, can be given in [ ] (square brackets).

$ grep 'ls -[lt]' script.sh

Matches 'ls -l' and 'ls -t' in the shell script, but ignores 'ls -a', 'ls -F' and other variations.

$ grep 'num[1-4]' myprog.pas   { range of possibles }

This would find the variables *num1*, *num2*, *num3* or *num4* in the program.

The search can be inverted – i.e. match everything except the given set of characters – by writing a caret (^) just inside the bracket.

$ grep '[^sf]printf' myprog.c   { not 's' or 'f' at the start }

Here **grep** would pass over lines containing 'sprintf' and 'fprintf', matching only the 'printf' lines in the C program.

Position

The caret (^) also has a second and quite different effect. If it is placed at the beginning of the string, it specifies that the match is to be sought at the beginnings of lines. Similarly, a dollar sign ($) at the end of a string points **grep** to the ends of lines.

```
$ grep '^do' *.c { line starts with 'do' }
$ grep 'pg$' *    { line ends with 'pg' }
```

By fixing the position, the '**^do**' expression will focus on the start of 'do .. while' loops in the C programs, but ignore most other occurrences of 'do'. The '**pg$**' search will likewise pass over those lines that started with 'pg' or used it as an intermediate pipe.

If you looking for one of these symbols – as a normal character – remove its special significance by prefixing it with the backslash (\).

```
$ grep '\$' *.txt
```

Now you can find that text about US currency.

Redirection

Don't forget that the output from any command can be redirected to a file, or sent for further processing through a pipe. Having tracked down the lines within files, you can then do something with them directly, rather than just view them on the screen.

```
$ grep alevel /etc/passwd >alevel.list
```

This would send the list of A level students to file, for later reference.

grep in pipes

Where you are going to get more than you really want, add a **grep** pipe to the end of the line to filter the output. For example, you want to know if Freddie is logged in, but there are a lot of users on the system. Rather than having to scan a lengthy output, get **grep** to do it for you:

```
$ who |grep freddie
freddietty14     Nov 18 10:49
```

Yes, he's there and has been working since 10:49.

egrep and fgrep

These two utilities are almost identical to **grep** but offer additional flexibility in the types of expressions that can be used. In different ways, each will allow you to specify more than one pattern in your search expression. With **egrep** you can build OR expressions, and with **fgrep** you can give a whole set of alternative patterns. The normal **grep** options work with them both.

In **egrep**, each pattern must be enclosed in (curved brackets), and separated by a vertical bar (|), with the whole expression enclosed in quotes.

This will pick out any lines that contain either 'John' or 'Jane'.

```
$ egrep '(John) | (Jane)' stafflist
```

fgrep will only work with fixed strings – no wildcards here. As this makes it a simpler routine, it runs faster than the standard **grep**. (On a decent system, you are unlikely to notice the difference unless you are searching through large directories stuffed with files.) Though the string patterns must be fixed, you can have any number of them in the search list. The separator here must be a newline (type the \ backslash then press [Enter]), and the whole set must be enclosed in quotes.

```
$ fgrep 'May \
June \
July \
August \
September' *.memo
```

Where you have a set of text items that you want to search for regularly, write them into a file, and use the **-f** option. Some system administrators use this method to scan the mailboxes for unacceptable words – including any references to the system administrator!

```
$ fgrep -f censor /usr/spool/mail/*
```

Saving space

pack – compress files

If a file is being put into cold storage, it may as well take as little disk space as possible. **pack** will compress a file, removing the original and replacing it by one with a **.z** extension. The degree of compression depends upon the type of file. Typically, **pack** will only manage a 15% saving on a compiled file, but 50% or more with text files.

● It is generally not worth trying to pack files of less than 2k, as the extra code needed to interpret the compression takes more space than that saved by packing. **pack** checks on possible saving, and will abandon the effort if it is not worthwhile.

● **pack** will not work with files that have long filenames. Unix only recognises the first 14 characters of a filename, and as the **.z** extension must be recognisable, for later unpacking, the original name cannot be more than 12 characters.

At the simplest, the command is simply followed by the name:

```
$ pack bigprog.pas
pack: bigprog.pas: 43.8% Compression
```

The packed file will be called 'bigprog.pas.z'.

pack options

-f forces the packing, even where there is no saving. This is mainly of value where you want to use a wildcard expression on a set of files, prior to putting them into cold storage.

Take note

pack works on a single file basis. You cannot **pack** a set of files into one compressed file. Merging them into a single file after compression would be ill-advised as there is no simple means to separate them again.

```
$ pack -f *.txt
$ mv *.z old
```

With this sequence, all text files will be compressed then moved into the *old* directory. Even with **-f** selected, **pack** will still fail on long filenames.

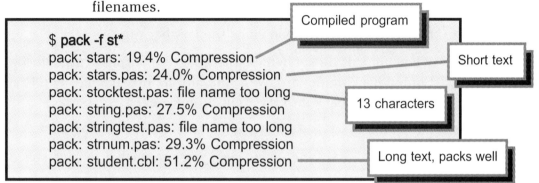

```
$ pack -f st*
pack: stars: 19.4% Compression
pack: stars.pas: 24.0% Compression
pack: stocktest.pas: file name too long
pack: string.pas: 27.5% Compression
pack: stringtest.pas: file name too long
pack: strnum.pas: 29.3% Compression
pack: student.cbl: 51.2% Compression
```

Compiled program

Short text

13 characters

Long text, packs well

If you want to keep the compressed files in one place, create a special directory and stick them in there, or read on and find out about **cpio**.

unpack – restore packed files

unpack restores your original file. When using it, you can omit the **.z** extension, as **unpack** will check for that anyway.

```
$ unpack network.txt
```

This will search for a file called 'network.txt.z', uncompress it into 'network.txt' and remove the compressed copy.

pcat – packed file concatenation

pcat is the **cat** equivalent for packed files. Use it to view, without unpacking, or redirect the output to save an unpacked copy without removing the compressed file.

```
$ pcat thing.pas          { view the file }
$ pcat funcs.c.z >funcs.c  { unpack but retain the packed file }
```

cpio – copy in and out

cpio is primarily for copying to and from archive (backup) files on tapes and floppy disks. It is an essential tool for system administrators, but has features which make it of interest to ordinary users.

- cpio can be used in conjunction with **find**, to copy selected files from locations throughout a directory structure – perhaps all those had been changed since the last backup.

- When you copy a *set* of files with **cpio**, the output is a single file. Copied back in, the archive splits into its original files and they are dropped back into the right directories.

- Individual files, or wildcard selections, can be copied back.

- If the **cpio** file is for cold storage, you can **pack** it to save space.

cpio is a complex command, with a large set of options. Fortunately, you can ignore most of them when you are copying to and from a file. To test it, go into your 'examples' directory, and check that this contains at least one sub-directory with some files in it. As things may go wrong when testing, these files should be dispensable! If necessary, create a new sub-directory and copy a few files into it. You might also like to create a new directory called 'archives', or something similar, up at the top level, parallel to 'examples'.

cpio options

-o selects **outward** copying. The list of files to be copied is piped in, usually from a **find** but sometimes from an **ls** command, and the output is redirected to the archive file. For example:

```
$ find . -print | cpio -o > backup.cpio
```

This **find** will locates all the files in the current and subordinate directories. **-print** will generate a list of filenames. These are fed into **cpio**, which archives them into a file called 'backup.cpio'. Try it in your 'examples' directory, then run an **ls** to make sure that it is there.

```
$ find . -ctime 0 -print | cpio -o > ../archives/dec15.bak
```

This time, **find** is being used selectively, and the output has been redirected to a file in the 'archives' directory.

-i selects **Inward** copying from an archive file. The files to be recovered from the archive are specified by a wildcard expression. As before, the archive file is redirected in. Try this to test the inwards copying. There should be several files starting with 'f' in the 'examples' directory. Remove one or two – but not all of them, then give the command:

```
$ cpio -i f* < backup.cpio
```

This will copy in those files starting with 'f' which have been removed, but will not normally overwrite existing files.

-u causes the inward copying to be **unconditional.** With this option set, archive files will overwrite existing ones of the same name. Try it. Edit one of your 'f...' files, and give this command:

```
$ cpio -iu f* <backup.cpio
```

Examine the relevant file. You should find that it is the earlier version.

-t creates a **Table of Contents** to show you what is in an archive. It must be used with the -i option, though it does not do any actual copying.

```
$ cpio -it < backup.cpio
```

-d Creates **Directories**. Use this to recreate a directory structure – either in a different part of the system, or because the original structure has been lost. **cpio** records a file's path along with the file. It can then use this to drop files into place – but only if the directories exist. With -d set, **cpio** creates directories if necessary. Check where you are in the syste before giving the command, so that the directories are created where they should be.

To test it out, clear the files from the 'dispensable' sub-directory, then remove the directory itself. Now try:

```
$ cpio -id <backup.cpio
```

Run an **ls** and you should find that the directory is back.

Finally, back to space-saving. Once you have archived your files, you can compress them, to give you a neat, compact 'cold-store'.

```
$ find . -ctime 0 -print | cpio -o >dec15.arc
$ pack dec15.arc
```

Summary

- ❑ A **simple directory structure** will make it easier to locate and organise your files

- ❑ With **find**, you can **track down a file** on the basis of its name, type, date of last edit and other properties. The found files can be listed on screen, or passed to another program for processing.

- ❑ **grep** will **search through text files** for a given string or wildcard expression. By setting it to search through sets of files, you can use grep to find ones that contain a key word or phrase.

- ❑ **grep wildcards** are different from those used in other shell commands.

- ❑ Use the **egrep** variation if you want to search for alternative patterns; use **fgrep** if you are searching for simple strings.

- ❑ Files which are no longer in regular use can be compressed with **pack** to save space.

- ❑ **cpio** will copy a set of files into a single **archive** – and restore them when needed. It is mainly used for backups but, combined with pack, can be used for the efficient long-term storage of old files.

7 Text file processing

Displaying text files

The sort of text file processing that we are looking at here is not processing in the sense of word-processing or otherwise preparing text for publication. There are Unix utilities that will do that, but they are not easy to use. If you want good-looking printed output, either turn to a specialised word-processing application on your Unix system, or switch to a PC and run your text through a desk-top publishing package. If these options are not available to you, and you still want to control the type styles and layout, then the System V Unix software does include a very sophisticated utility that will do it. It's called **nroff**, and you can read all about it in the users' manuals.

What we will be covering in this chapter are those simpler, but useful commands that will process text files either as wholes or in large chunks. The more detailed 'cut and paste' utilities will be dealt with in the next chapter.

cat – concatenate and display files

cat can be used in several different formats:

cat *files*

Displays the files on screen. '*files*' can be one or any number of files, though as they are run together without any break, you would rarely **cat** more than one at a time to the screen.

cat > *newfile*

Redirects input from the keyboard to the file, *newfile*.

cat >> *oldfile*

Redirects input from the keyboard and appends it to the end of *oldfile*.

cat *files* > *newfile*   { join files to make new one }

Con**cat**enates (the origin of the name!) two or more *files* to create a single *newfile*.

cat *files* >> *oldfile*

Appends any number of *files* to the end of *oldfile*.

cat options

-v Make non-printing characters visible

The screen can only handle safely the letters, digits and symbols that make up the core of the ASCII set (characters 32 to 126). Characters outside this range will have special effects, that vary from terminal to terminal. Character 7 will make the terminal 'beep', another will clear the screen, others will move the cursor, turn on the highlight, or even turn off the terminal!

If a file is from a word-processor, it may have codes to control the printer – selecting fonts, setting line spacing, margins and the like. If it is a data file, the numbers may be in machine format, rather than as strings of digits. Send files like this to the screen with a simple **cat** and the results will be unpredictable. Use the **-v** option and the non-printing characters will be made visible in the form ^C. This refers to the key which, if you pressed it while holding [Ctrl], would create that character. For example, the end-of-file character is [Ctrl]-[Z] and would show up with **cat -v** as ^Z.

The simple print control characters – tab, carriage return and line feed – are processed as normal even with the **-v** option on.

-s Suppress error messages

If you tell **cat** to print a file and it can't find it, then **cat** will tell you so. This is all well and good most of the time, but within a shell program you might prefer to suppress the error message.

-e Print End of Line marker

This can only be used in combination with **-v**. It puts '$' at the end of each line. It will therefore show up trailing spaces and help to identify those logical lines that occupy more than one line on the screen.

cat works well for displaying small files, but as it pours text through in a continual stream, it is not convenient for anything that runs to more than one screen. For larger files, you are better off with **pg**, which we will get to in a moment, or **head** or **tail**.

head

head is a handy, but often over-looked, little utility. It displays the top end – normally the first 10 lines – of a file.

Check it out with any lengthy file. If you want to create one quickly, redirect the listing from a big directory, like 'bin', into a file.

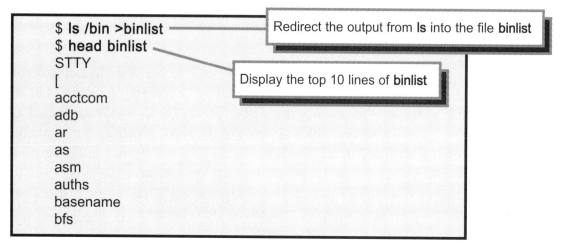

```
$ ls /bin >binlist
$ head binlist
STTY
[
acctcom
adb
ar
as
asm
auths
basename
bfs
```

Redirect the output from ls into the file binlist

Display the top 10 lines of binlist

If 10 lines is too many or too few for you, set the number of lines you want by giving the number as an option after the command:

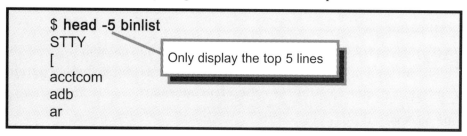

```
$ head -5 binlist
STTY
[
acctcom
adb
ar
```

Only display the top 5 lines

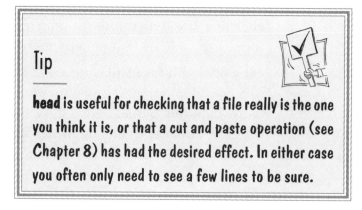

Tip

head is useful for checking that a file really is the one you think it is, or that a cut and paste operation (see Chapter 8) has had the desired effect. In either case you often only need to see a few lines to be sure.

tail

tail solves the big file problem from the other end, though this has a little more to it. The basic command takes the same format:

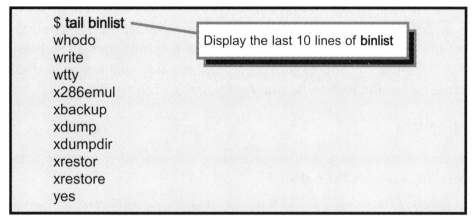

The default display is of the last 10 lines, but the starting place can be changed. You can either count from the top of the file, indicated by **+n**, or from the bottom (**-n**), where 'n' is the number of lines. In either case, **tail** will display from there to the end of the file. There is no way to specify an earlier end. For example:

$ **tail +50 myprog.c**
$ **tail -5 herprog.c**

The first starts at line 50, the second 5 lines from the end.

By default **tail** works in lines, but it can be in characters (indicated by the letter **c)** or in blocks of 512 characters (indicated by **b**). The letter must be written after the +/- start place specifier. For example:

$ **tail -100 c letter.text**

Give you the last 100 characters of 'letter.txt'.

$ **tail +3 b bigfile.data**

Gives you the third and subsequent blocks of 'bigfile.data'.

pg – the file viewer

So far we have used **pg** simply for reading through a file one page at a time, but **pg** is a fully-fledged file-viewing utility. It enables you to move backwards and forwards through a file, leap to a specified place, search for a string of text or switch between several files. The controls for this work at two levels. The command line options set the basic nature of the viewing environment, and the internlal controls used while **pg** is running handle the switch and search facilities.

Command line options

-c clears the screen before printing each new page, rather than scrolling up from the bottom.

-*number* selects how many lines to display at a time. The default is one less than the screen height. Do not confused this with ...

+*number*, which specifies the line at which to start viewing, e.g.

$ **pg +50 -20 longfile**

This pages through 'longfile', 20 lines at a time, starting at line 50.

+/*pattern*/ starts the display at the first line containing a matching string. The *pattern* follows the same rules as in **grep**. This is handy. Having used **grep** to locate a text item, you can then view it with **pg**. There's a string to number conversion function in one of my Pascal programs. Where is it and what does it look like? I think I called it 'str_to_num' or something similar:

```
$ grep 'str.*num' *.pas      { starts with 'str' ends with 'num' }
calc.pas:function str_num(str:string; base:integer):integer;
calc.pas:  str_num := num;
calc.pas:   value := str_num(s,b);
```

calc.pas is a long program. I can leap to the relevant section and display 15 lines, which should be enough, with the **pg** command line:

```
$ pg -15 +/str_num/ calc.pas
function str_num(str:string; base:integer):integer;
var
...
...
```

-p *string* defines a new **prompt** for the internal controls, instead of ':'. Display the current page number in the prompt by the special combination '%d'. For really smart paging, combine this with ...

-s, (short for '**standout**') which highlights the prompt and any messages. e.g.

> $ pg -p 'Page %d :' -s mytext

This will give you a bright, clear page number at the bottom of the screen, and knowing that number can be useful.

Internal controls

While **pg** is sending text to the screen, [Ctrl]-[D], [Del] or [^] will stop the flow and bring up the **pg** prompt. All the other commands are given in response to that prompt. They fall into three groups.

Movement

This can be either absolute or relative, and is usually measured in pages. Give a number by itself to leap to a chosen page. Put a + or - in front to move forwards or backwards a set number of pages. If you want to move by lines, rather than pages, write 'l' (letter L) after the number, for example:

> : 3   { go to page 3 }
> : 25 l   { display from line 25 onwards }
> : +2   { skip 2 pages forward }
> : -10 l   { scroll back 10 lines }

There are two other movement commands.

. (dot)   redisplays the current page

$ leaps to the last screenful.

Take note

The $ control may have unexpected results if you are using **pg** in a pipe.

Search

The internal search uses the same pattern formats (the **ed/grep** standards) as the command line option. A simple search for the next occurrence of the word 'function', for instance, would take the form:

: /function/

The nature of the operation can be controlled in three ways. You can search backwards by replacing the /slashes/ with ?question marks?. You can jump to a particular occurrence of a string by writing a number at the start of the command. Finally, you can tack an **m** to the end to set the display so that the line containing the matching string is at the middle of the screen, or a **b** to place it at the bottom.

: 2/function/	{ go to the 2nd match, from the current page }
: ?'char c'?	{ go back and find 'char c' }
: /meeting/ m	{ find 'meeting' and display in mid-screen }

File Handling

s *filename* saves the current file. This is not as pointless as it may sound. If you are using **pg** in a pipe, this gives you the option of retaining data that would be otherwise only sent to the screen. If you are using it to scan a set of old files, then this option lets you make a new copy as you work your way through.

If you have started **pg** with a list of files, you can close down the current file and jump on or back to a different one. Note that you are working by their *position in the list of files*, not the filenames. The commands take the form of a number followed by **n** for 'next' or **p** for 'previous'. Suppose that you had started with the command line:

$ **pg chap1.txt chap2.txt chap3.txt chap4.txt chap5.txt**

You have paged through to *chap3.txt*, each file coming into view as the previous ends. You now want to view a different file.

: 2p	{ go back 2, to **chap1.txt** }
: 1n	{ go on to next file, jumping out of the current one }

split

This takes a file and sub-divides it into a set of files of fixed length. (The original file stays intact.) This is a crude but quick way to reduce a large file to manageable chunks.

The new files are labelled with a two-letter appendage to their name, starting with **aa** and going up to **zz**. If you do not specify otherwise, the files will be called *xaa*, *xab*, *xac*, etc, and they will be 1000 lines long. A different length and an alternative filename can be specified.

For example, to divide *bigprog.lst*, a sizable error report produced when trying to compile a Cobol program, into 40-line segments whose names start with *bigbit*, you would use the line:

    $ split -40 bigprog.lst bigbit

This gives you *bigbitaa*, *bigbitab*, *bigbitac* and the like. You can now run these out to the printer, leaving deep bottom margins for notes:

    $ lp bigbit*

(Your system may well use an alternative to **lp** to send output to a specific printer.)

This simple division by length is rarely of much practical use. It is generally more useful to divide into logical sections, based on content. For that you need **csplit**.

csplit – spilt files by context

This splits files on the basis of key words – or rather, **grep** expressions that generate key words or phrases. It can also do a simple split based on line count, or a combination of the two. Like **split** it produces a set of files where the names share a common base, though here the part-identifiers are numbers. The default names are xx00, xx01, xx02, etc.

The command takes the form:

    csplit [options] *source_file key1 key2* ...

The file is split so that the first of the resulting files runs from the start to the line before the first key, and each key word is in the first line of a new section. Obviously, to split a file successfully by key words, you need to know where the words are. If you have to read the text to find out where to split, you may as well use the block write facilities of **vi** or of another word-processor. In practice, most **csplit**s would be based on section headings in text files or procedure labels in programs.

To see it at work, let's take this summary of a recent White Paper. (Write your own with **vi**– it'll be good yank and paste practice.)

```
woffle
woffle
Proposals
blah
blah
blah
Summary
rhubarb
rhubarb
rhubarb

$ csplit paper /Proposals/ /Summary/
14
25
32
```

Note that the key expressions are each enclosed in /slashes/. As we have given no base filenames, the default 'xx..' forms are used. The numbers that are printed at the end of the operation, are the character counts for each of the new files.

```
$ cat xx00
woffle
woffle
$ cat xx01
Proposals          { the first key word }
blah
blah
blah
$ cat xx02
Summary            { the next key word }
rhubarb
rhubarb
rhubarb
```

csplit options

There are three options, which can be used alone or in combination.

-s Suppresses the character count display on completion;

-k Keeps the files created up to that point if an error causes the command to stop. These would normally be wiped as **csplit** takes an all-or-nothing approach.

-f *name* sets a basename for the new files.

Test them. Give a filename, and write an error into the line so that the command will fail.

```
$ csplit -k -f cutting paper /Proposals/ /Conclusion/
14
/Conclusion/ - out of range
70
```

That 'out of range' error tells us that **csplit** reached the end of the file without finding a match for the string. View the new files, and you will see that the second includes everything from 'Proposals' to the end.

```
$ cat cutting01
Proposals
blah
....
rhubarb
rhubarb
```

csplit arguments

So far we have only used simple string expressions to split the file, but there are three other possibilities here.

Enclose the string in **%percent%** signs and **csplit** does not write the section that is ended by that expression.

```
$ csplit paper /Proposals/ %Summary%
```

This will give you two files – the first few lines, up to 'Proposals', and the last section from 'Summary' onwards.

According to the Manual, **csplit** can take two types of numeric argument. In theory, if you give a **number**, by itself, that will split off a file containing that number of lines, starting from the current position; while a number enclosed in {curly brackets} will repeat the previous argument for that number of times:

$ csplit -k bigfile 50 {100}

This should split 'bigfile' into 50-line segments. (The '-k' option ensures that if there are less than 100 segments, those that have been created are kept when the command terminates.)

In practice, on the (SCO System V) installation used for testing commands for this book, **csplit** behaves in a different way – the **man** entry notwithstanding. The {number} arguments are simply ignored, while plain numbers are treated as absolute line references. Thus:

$ csplit bigfile 50

splits the file into two segments; the first running from line 1 to 49, the second from line 50 onwards.

$ csplit bigfile 50 150 300

This would split the file into 4 segments, containing lines 1-49, 50-149, 150-299 and 300 to the end. Test yours carefully before using this command in earnest.

csplit in pipes

With most commands, the input filename is omitted when the command is used in a pipeline. With **csplit**, you must write a dash in place of the filename.

> ### Tip
>
> If your mail system sets a maximum size for messages – many do – and you want to send someone a large file, use **split** to chop it into acceptable-size chunks.

wc – word counter

This utility is probably of most use to journalist and students – or anyone else who gets paid or marked by the word! It will tell you the number of lines, words and characters in a file. A 'word' is defined as a string of characters separated from the next by a space, tab or newline. It may therefore give slightly odd results with some program text files – but as the number of words in a program is usually irrelevant, that shouldn't matter.

Create a decent-sized file by running a long listing from the 'bin' into a file, then pass that to **wc**:

```
$ ls -l /bin >longbin
$ wc longbin
152   1361   8802 longbin
```

The first count is of lines, the next of words and the last of characters. You can have any one or two of these figure alone by setting the options **-l** for lines, **-w** for words and **-c** for characters:

```
$ wc -l longbin
152 longbin
$ wc -w longbin
1361 longbin
```

As elsewhere, the file specification can include wildcards. For a full breakdown of a directory, try:

```
$ wc -l *
6 add.c
61 bubble.pas
3 fax
12 filelist
164 Fincert.txt
134 sarah.let
3 fox
12 intest.pas
7 sum.c
1 temp
433 total
```

spell – spelling checker

spell is a quick and efficient spelling checker. The dictionary is extensive, but has the usual limitations over proper names and specialised terms. It is not difficult to add your own supplementary list and link it into the checker. A simple **spell**, followed by the filename, will produce a list of words that it cannot recognise.

```
$ spell memo
Heinemann
arguement
seperately
thier
```

The list is arranged in ASCII order, which is very tidy, but not very helpful in terms of locating the errors within the file. Unfortunately there is no option which will give you the line numbers to assist in later editing. There is a simple solution to this problem. Redirect the output from **spell** into a file, then pass it to **fgrep** which can give you the context and line number.

```
$ spell memo >errors
$ fgrep -n -f errors memo        { -n for line numbers }
47:specialised word-processing application on thier Unix system
171:can take two types of numeric arguement. In theory, if you
205:There are three options, which can be used seperately or in
480:the well-known international publishers, Heinemann, whose
```

With a long file, the whole process may take a few moments. Improve your efficiency by combining the two commands into a single line, running the lot in the background and sending the final output to a file. The line is then:

```
$ (spell memo > errors ; fgrep -n -f errors memo >errlist ) &
```

You can then check the 'errlist' file later, and in the meantime can get on with other pressing jobs.

An alternative, or complementary, approach is to run the two commands together in a shell script. Using 'errors' as a standard name for the error list, your script should look like this:

```
spell $1 > errors        { $1 will collect the filename }
fgrep -n -f errors $1     { and pass it to fgrep }
```

There are two that are really useful:

-b selects **British** spelling

+*filename* makes **spell** cross-check with your own supplementary word list. This is a plain text file, containing one word on each line, sorted into simple ASCII order.

To create your supplementary dictionary, collect **spell**'s output into an 'errors' file, each time you use it. Edit the file to remove any real errors, then **cat** the filtered list to the end of your permanent supplementary file – perhaps called *wordlist*. This must be sorted into order. *wordlist* can then be included in your command line next time you use **spell**.

```
$ cat errors >> wordlist          { append to supplementary file }
$ sort wordlist                   { see Chapter 8 for sort }
....
$ spell +wordlist textfile > errors   { next time round }
```

Take note

Unless you specify otherwise, **spell** uses American spelling.

Summary

- ❏ **cat** will display one or more text files on screen, or – using redirection – **concatenate them into one new file**.

- ❏ If you just want to see the **top few lines** of a file, use your **head**.

- ❏ **tail** will **display the end**, or a selected part, of a text file.

- ❏ If you want to **view**, but not edit, a long text file, use **pg**. Its commands will let you move through the file or search for words.

- ❏ **Large files can be broken down** into segments with **split**.

- ❏ **wc**, the word counter, will tell you **how many words**, lines and characters there are in a file.

- ❏ You can **spell check** a file with **spell**.

8 Data file processing

Databases

In Chapter 6, I touched on the idea of using Unix for data file processing, when introducing **grep**. You saw that, by finding lines that contained matching strings, **grep** could select records from a database. Let's look at the database concept and at some of the utilities that can manipulate data files in other ways.

Even if you are not interested in databases, read on. The commands and techniques covered below can be applied to any organised files, and there are plenty of those in a Unix system.

Before we go any further, we should create some suitable files, so that we have something to work on. To be suitable, a file should have one record per line, with the fields separated by 'white space' – i.e. one or more space characters or tabs. The basic shape can be seen as:

	Field 0	Field 1	Field 2	Field 3	Field 4
Record 1					
Record 2					
Record 3					
Record 4					
...					

Such a file might, for example, hold stock data. Each record would hold the information for one type of goods, and the fields would be Reference Number, Description, Supplier Reference, Quantity in Stock, Warehouse Location, and whatever. In a college, lecturers might use a database to store students' marks.

There are many databases in a Unix system. The '/etc/passwd' file is a good example. Each line holds the essential data on a user – username, ID, group, proper name, home directory, and login shell. Within every directory you will find another database – the file that holds the index to the directory. You can't see it, but you can get at its contents by simply typing **ls**. A full listing has the classic database structure and will be ideal for demonstrating the use of data processing commands. Go to one of your smaller directories – half a dozen files or so will do nicely – and create a working copy of the listing with this:

```
$ ls -l > filelist                          Collect the list in a file
$ cat filelist                                           Have a look at it
total 12
-rwx------  1 mac staff        4929 Nov 28 17:29  Fincert.txt
-rw-r--r--  1 mac staff         400 Mar 18 10:57  Temp
-rw-r--r--  1 mac staff          58 Nov 28 17:28  add.c
-rwx------  1 mac staff         986 Nov 28 17:28  bubble.pas
-rw-r--r--  1 mac staff          92 Oct 18 15:44  fax
-rw-r--r--  1 mac staff           0 Nov 28 17:30  filelist
-rw-r--r--  1 mac staff         689 Nov 15 12:20  sarah.let
-rw-r--r--  1 mac staff          92 Oct 18 15:44  fox
-rw-r--r--  1 mac staff         171 Nov 28 17:28  intest.pas
-rw-r--r--  1 mac staff          62 Nov 28 17:28  sum.c
```

(Use **vi** to edit out the 'total' line. Its presence will only confuse matters.)

Each record has nine fields – permissions, links, owner, group, size, month, day, time and name. In those commands that allow you to specify fields, they are identified by number, counting from 0 on the left. Here, for instance, field 4 is the file size.

We will want a second file later, and one where the separator is not the standard white space. This is the case with '/etc/passwd', though it may have far more than we need for example purposes. Use **grep** to slice out the records of one of the smaller groups on your system.

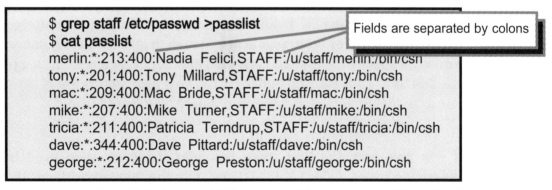

```
$ grep staff /etc/passwd >passlist
$ cat passlist                                  Fields are separated by colons
merlin:*:213:400:Nadia  Felici,STAFF:/u/staff/merlin:/bin/csh
tony:*:201:400:Tony  Millard,STAFF:/u/staff/tony:/bin/csh
mac:*:209:400:Mac  Bride,STAFF:/u/staff/mac:/bin/csh
mike:*:207:400:Mike  Turner,STAFF:/u/staff/mike:/bin/csh
tricia:*:211:400:Patricia  Terndrup,STAFF:/u/staff/tricia:/bin/csh
dave:*:344:400:Dave  Pittard:/u/staff/dave:/bin/csh
george:*:212:400:George  Preston:/u/staff/george:/bin/csh
```

Your '/etc/passwd' file may not be structured in quite the same way. The important point for our purposes is that the fields are separated by something other than white space – here the separator is the colon.

sort – sort into order

By default, **sort** arranges the file into ASCII order, taking as its key the whole line, and sends its output to the screen. As it works on the ASCII sequence, all capitals come before lower case letters and numbers as treated as digits not values. And as it works on the whole line, the simple **sort** is not much use unless the key field happens to be the first. However, just to show how easy **sort** is to use – if the default settings apply – try it now with your 'filelist':

```
$ sort filelist
-rw-r--r--  1 mac staff            0 Nov 28 17:30 filelist
-rw-r--r--  1 mac staff          171 Nov 28 17:28 intest.pas
-rw-r--r--  1 mac staff          400 Mar 18 10:57 Temp
-rw-r--r--  1 mac staff           58 Nov 28 17:28 add.c
-rw-r--r--  1 mac staff           62 Nov 28 17:28 sum.c
-rw-r--r--  1 mac staff          689 Nov 15 12:20 sarah.let
-rw-r--r--  1 mac staff           92 Oct 18 15:44 fax
-rw-r--r--  1 mac staff           92 Oct 18 15:44 fox
-rwx------  1 mac staff         4929 Nov 28 17:29 Fincert.txt
```

Check your output and you should see a similar pattern. The order is determined firstly by the permissions – though these will be largely the same on all files – and then after that by file size. But look at the effect of sorting numbers by their ASCII codes, rather than values. '400' comes before '62'!

In most sorting operations, you will want the order to be determined by one or more specific fields. These may be in a group, scattered across the record or both, so it is not enough to give the field number. You must specify the first and last field number in each set. These are marked by a '+' for the first and '-' for the next field after the sort keys. For example, to sort on fields 2 and 3 only, you would use:

    sort +2 -4...

If you give only the first, then the later fields are also used to determine order; likewise, by setting only the 'next-after' field, the sort will use all the fields up to that point.

So, for a single field sort, you need something like this:

```
$ sort +5 -6 filelist
-rw-r--r--  1 mac staff              400 Mar 18 10:57 Temp
-rw-r--r--  1 mac staff                0 Nov 28 17:30 filelist
-rwx------  1 mac staff             4929 Nov 28 17:29 Fincert.txt
-rw-r--r--  1 mac staff              171 Nov 28 17:28 intest.pas
-rw-r--r--  1 mac staff               62 Nov 28 17:28 sum.c
-rw-r--r--  1 mac staff              689 Nov 15 12:20 sarah.let
-rw-r--r--  1 mac staff               58 Nov 28 17:28 add.c
-rw-r--r--  1 mac staff               92 Oct 18 15:44 fax
-rw-r--r--  1 mac staff               92 Oct 18 15:44 fox
```

This sorts alphabetically by month, field 5. To sort by month and then by name, you would have to specify fields 5 and 8, giving the command line:

$ **sort +5 -6 +8 filelist**

No 'next-after' field specification is needed for field 8, as there are no later fields.

If necessary, you can define the start and end more closely by specifying character positions within the fields. If you wanted to make the **minutes** a key in sorting the filelist, you would use:

$ **sort -n +7.3 -8 filelist**

sort then skips over the first three characters of the time field to pick up the minutes at position 3.

sort options

-f Folds upper to lower case to produce a true alphabetical sort. Do you have a mixture of capitals and lower case in the names in your *filelist*? If not, create a couple of new files (copying an existing one is the quickest way to do this) to give you a mixture, then run off a new version.

Use -f to sort file into alphabetic order of the filenames – field 8:

```
$ sort +8 filelist
-rw-r--r--  1 mac staff                   58 Nov 28 17:28 add.c
-rw-r--r--  1 mac staff                   92 Oct 18 15:44 fax
-rw-r--r--  1 mac staff                    0 Nov 28 17:30 filelist
-rwx------  1 mac staff                 4929 Nov 28 17:29 Fincert.txt
-rw-r--r--  1 mac staff                   92 Oct 18 15:44 fox
-rw-r--r--  1 mac staff                  171 Nov 28 17:28 intest.pas
-rw-r--r--  1 mac staff                  689 Nov 15 12:20 sarah.let
-rw-r--r--  1 mac staff                   62 Nov 28 17:28 sum.c
-rw-r--r--  1 mac staff                  400 Mar 18 10:57 Temp
```

-n Treats **numbers** as values. With this option, we can do a proper sort by filesize. Set the option, then specify the field:

```
$ sort -n +4 -5 filelist
-rw-r--r--  1 mac staff                    0 Nov 28 17:30 filelist
-rw-r--r--  1 mac staff                   58 Nov 28 17:28 add.c
-rw-r--r--  1 mac staff                   62 Nov 28 17:28 sum.c
-rw-r--r--  1 mac staff                   92 Oct 18 15:44 fax
-rw-r--r--  1 mac staff                   92 Oct 18 15:44 fox
-rw-r--r--  1 mac staff                  171 Nov 28 17:28 intest.pas
-rw-r--r--  1 mac staff                  400 Mar 18 10:57 Temp
-rw-r--r--  1 mac staff                  689 Nov 15 12:20 sarah.let
-rwx------  1 mac staff                 4929 Nov 28 17:29 Fincert.txt
```

-M (Notice the capital) sorts by **Month**. It first forces the characters in the field to capitals, then sorts in order 'JAN' to 'DEC'. It works equally well with abbreviations and full month names. Combine this with a numeric sort on the day field to put 'filelist' into date order:

```
$ sort -M +5 -6 -n +6 -7 filelist
-rw-r--r--  1 mac staff                  400 Mar 18 10:57 Temp
-rw-r--r--  1 mac staff                   92 Oct 18 15:44 fox
-rw-r--r--  1 mac staff                   92 Oct 18 15:44 fax
-rw-r--r--  1 mac staff                  689 Nov 15 12:20 sarah.let
-rw-r--r--  1 mac staff                    0 Nov 28 17:30 filelist
-rw-r--r--  1 mac staff                   58 Nov 28 17:28 add.c
-rw-r--r--  1 mac staff                   62 Nov 28 17:28 sum.c
-rw-r--r--  1 mac staff                  171 Nov 28 17:28 intest.pas
-rwx------  1 mac staff                 4929 Nov 28 17:29 Fincert.txt
```

-o *filename* Sends **output** to the named file – though as elsewhere, redirection can be used to create files. If there is an existing file of the given name, it will be overwritten. This line will create a new file, sorted in alphabetical order of the filenames – field 8.

```
$ sort -o sortfile -f +8 filelist
```

-t*char* Sets *char* as the **separator**, instead of white space. For this example, we will use 'passlist', generated from the '/etc/passwd' file, where the separator is a colon and spaces have no special significance. Write the new separator immediately after the '**-t**'.

```
$ sort -t: -n +2 -3 passlist
tony:*:201:400:Tony  Millard,STAFF:/u/staff/tony:/bin/csh
mike:*:207:400:Mike  Turner,STAFF:/u/staff/mike:/bin/csh
mac:*:209:400:Mac  Bride,STAFF:/u/staff/mac:/bin/csh
tricia:*:211:400:Patricia  Terndrup,STAFF:/u/staff/tricia:/bin/csh
george:*:212:400:George  Preston:/u/staff/george:/bin/csh
merlin:*:213:400:Nadia  Felici,STAFF:/u/staff/merlin:/bin/csh
dave:*:344:400:Dave  Pittard:/u/staff/dave:/bin/csh
```

-r Reverses the sort order. It can be used by itself or in combination with '**-f**' or '**-n**'. Try it, combined it with '**-n**' to sort 'filelist' into order of size, with the largest first:

```
$ sort -r -n +5 -6 -o filesize filelist
```

Take note

The order of options is largely irrelevant. All that really matters is that command starts with sort and ends with the input filename. These lines would all work just as well:

```
$ sort -n +5 -6 -r -o filesize filelist
$ sort -o filesize -r -n +5 -6 filelist
$ sort -r -o filesize -n +5 -6 filelist
```

cut – cut vertically through a file

This command is designed to cut fields out of a database, but will also slice a column of characters, of any width, out of a text file. It has two distinct modes of operation, working either by characters or by fields.

cut is basically straightforward, though a couple of minor alterations in its design would have made it easier to use.

- **cut**, unlike **sort**, does not recognise 'white space' (any string of spaces or a tab) as a field separator. The default separator for **cut** is the tab. You can specify an alternative character as the separator – but only a single character. As a result, if you have two fields separated by a string of spaces there's no way you can get it to skip over those spaces. This doesn't actually stop you from slicing space-separated files, but you have to tackle them differently.

- In **cut**, the fields are numbered from 1, not 0. It is a trivial difference, but if they had been the same in these respects, the techniques used with **sort** could have been carried over to **cut**, and vice versa – and you would make fewer errors with them both.

cut options are not particularly complex, but they are interdependent and we will tackle them as we come to them. Note that there is no option for output to file. The results will normally appear on the screen or be piped on to another command. If you do want to store the output, use the > redirect to send it to a file.

Cutting by fields

The -f option is used here. If the fields are tab-separated, then the command takes the form:

cut -f *field-list file*

The *field-list* can contain single field numbers – counting from 1, or ranges. The fields in the list are separated by commas. For example, to cut field 3 and those between 6 and 10 from a file called 'mydata':

$ **cut -f 3,6-10 mydata**

If the file uses an alternative separator character, define this with the **-d** option. Test the option with your 'passlist' file, where the separator is the colon:

```
$ cut -d: -f5,1,7 ../passlist
merlin:Nadia Felici,STAFF:/bin/csh
tony:Tony Millard,STAFF:/bin/csh
mac:Mac Bride,STAFF:/bin/csh
mike:Mike Turner,STAFF:/bin/csh
tricia:Patricia Terndrup,STAFF:/bin/csh
dave:Dave Pittard:/bin/csh
george:George Preston:/bin/csh
```

The order in which fields are listed is unimportant. Whatever order you use, the output will always be in field order. You can see that here, where the input list was 5, 1, 7, the output is in the order 1, 5, 7.

If a line has no separator characters in it, it is normally output intact. This can be useful as it means that table headings and annotation lines are carried across from the original file. These would not occur in most datafiles, but are found in files that are themselves reports from a database. If you want to suppress these, use the **-s** option, e.g.

```
$ cut -s -f3-5,7 mydata.rpt
```

This cuts fields 3 to 5 and field 7 from the report, and also removes any header lines.

Cutting by position

This option is selected by **-c**, and is the way to deal with files that are separated by spaces, as long as the spacing is such that the data for each field starts and ends in an identifiable column. This is the case with our 'filelist' example. Identifying the columns can be a bit of a bother. The best bet may well be to load it into **vi** or a word-processor. Most have a status line that displays the row and column position of the cursor, so by moving the cursor along a line, you can read off the appropriate column numbers. At worst, you can move the cursor one character at a time and count!

```
0          1          2          3          4          5          6
12345678901234567890123456789012345678901234567890123456789012345
-rw-r--r--    1 mac    staff               0 Nov 28 17:30    filelist
-rw-r--r--    1 mac    staff             171 Oct 29  14:32   intest.pas
-rw-r--r--    1 mac    staff             400 Mar 18 10:57    Temp
-rw-r--r--    1 mac    staff              62 Nov 10 13:49    sum.c
-rw-r--r--    1 mac    staff             689 Nov 15 12:20    sarah.let
-rw-r--r--    1 mac    staff              58 Nov 20 14:05    add.c
-rw-r--r--    1 mac    staff              92 Oct 18 15:44    fax
-rw-r--r--    1 mac    staff              92 Oct 18 15:44    fox
-rwx------    1 mac    staff            4929 Nov 28 17:29    Fincert.txt
```

Suppose we wanted to cut the filesize and names out of 'filelist'. We can work out that the filesizes all fit between columns 35 and 40, and that the names start at column 54 and run to 65. (Yours may well be different – the positions largely depend upon the tab settings of your terminal.)

```
$ cut -c35-40,54-65 filelist
4929 Fincert.txt
400 Temp
58 add.c
92 fax
0 filelist
92 fox
171 intest.pas
689 sarah.let
62 sum.c
```

That space between the sizes and names is there because it was included in the specification for the name cut. If its position had been given as 55-65, i.e. starting at the first letter of the name, there would have been no space.

As with the field-based option, this cut outputs its sets of characters in the same order as they were in the original file, no matter how you list them in the command line. If you want to cut columns and rearrange their order, the answer is to cut each one into a separate file, them splice them back together with **paste** (see page 140).

cut them now, and you will be ready for **paste** when we get to it in a moment. Redirect the filesizes to a file called 'sizes', the dates and times to 'dates', and the names to one called 'names'.

```
$ cut -c35-40 filelist > sizes
$ cut -c42-53 filelist > dates
$ cut -c54-65 filelist > names
```

cut works well in pipes, as long as you know the field structure of the output of the previous command. For example, you could find the login IDs and full names of all the Pauls on your system by this combination of **grep** and **cut**.

```
$ grep -i paul /etc/passwd | cut -d: -f 1,5
pixi:Paul McGovern,NDCS2B
cleric:Paul Burnett,NDCS2B
hawk:Paul Godden,NDCS1A
pelican:Paul Taylor,NDCS1B
earth:Paul Hannan,NCCS1A
asteroid:Paul McMullen,NCCS1IT
silkcut:Paul Smith,NDITA1
```

paste – merge files by column

At the simplest, this takes a number of files, each consisting of a column of text, and arranges them side by side. For example, to produce a list of filenames followed by their sizes, we would use:

```
$ paste names sizes
Fincert.txt 4929
Temp        400
add.c       58
fax         92
filelist    0
fox         92
intest.pas  171
sarah.let   689
sum.c       62
```

The result may well not be as neat as this! The pasted columns here are separated by tabs, the default separator. As a result, if an item in the first column overruns a tab position, the corresponding item in the second column will be pushed to the next tab position. If you want to produce a file for print-out, then a little work with **vi** or a word-processor may be necessary.

paste options

-d *list* **Defines** an alternative set of separators. With this option the command takes the form:

paste -d *list* file1 file2 file...

The *list* is a set of one or more characters to be used – one at a time – as separators. When **paste** reaches the end of the list, it cycles back to the start and runs through them again. The end of each line is always terminated by a newline, no matter what characters you use in the list. Any characters can be used, but note the special escape combinations:

\\t	tab space
\\n	newline
\\	backslash
\\0	null string – i.e. no separator

140

The characters here are those recognised by the C language. Note the double slashes! The backslash has a special meaning to the shell (it 'escapes' the following character), so to get it past the shell and through to the **paste** command, it must itself be escaped. The first backslash is then stripped off by the shell, and the second one gives 't', 'n' and '0' their special meanings in **paste**. To paste together our sample files in the order date, name and size, with a colon after the date and a tab after the name, we would need the line:

```
$ paste -d:\\t dates names sizes
Nov 27 17:29: Fincert.txt    4929
Mar 18 10:57: Temp           400
Nov 10 14:05: add.c          58
Mar 18 10:57: fax            92
Nov 28 17:28: filelist       0
Nov 28 17:28: fox            92
Oct 29 14:32: intest.pas     171
Nov 15 12:20: sarah.let      689
Nov 10 13:49: sum.c          62
```

-s Pastes **successive** lines across the screen. With this option you can break one long list down into a set of columns, to make it fit more compactly on screen or paper. Use 'binlist' – the file created by redirecting the **ls** listing from the '\bin' – or any other suitable file. **paste** it across the screen with:

```
$ paste -s binlist
STTY      acctcom   adb       ar        as        asm       auths
basename  bfs       cat       cc        chgrp     chkshlib  chmod
chown     chroot    clear     cmp       conv      convert   copy
cp        cpio      cprs      csh       date      dd        df
diff      dirname   dis       dos       dparam    dtype     du
dump      echo      ed        env       expr      false     login
lorder    lr        ls        lx        mail      make      masm
mc68k     mesg      mkdir     mkshlib   mt        mv        ncheck
newgrp    nice      nm        nohup     od        passwd    pdp11
pr        printenv  ps        pstat     pwd       ranlib    rcc
red       rm        rmdir     rsh       sddate    sed       setkey
setpgrp   whodo     write     wtty      x286emul  xbackup   xdump
xdumpdir  xrestor   xrestore  yes
```

141

Unlike the simple **paste**, the -s version does not put newlines at the end of each line across. This doesn't matter on screen, but if you pasting to a file that will be printed, it can play havoc with the layout on paper. In this situation, decide how many columns you would like then supply a list of tabs and newlines with the **-d** option. For example, for a four-column layout of the **\bin** list, you would use:

```
$ paste -s -d\\t\\t\\t\\n binlist
STTY        [           acctcom  adb
ar          as          asm      auths
....
who         whodo       write    wtty
x286emul    xbackup     xdump    xdumpdir
xrestor     xrestore    yes
```

Multiple files and multiple columns

If you use **-s** with more than one file, it pastes the first file into columns, then starts the second on a new line below it. This is probably not as you would like it, as it destroys any links between the items in the files. If you did want to paste two files and arrange them in, say, three pairs of columns across the page, then it would take two operations. These can be run on two separate lines - the first to create an intermediate two-column file; the second to split this into three columns. The separator list will require two tabs and a newline.

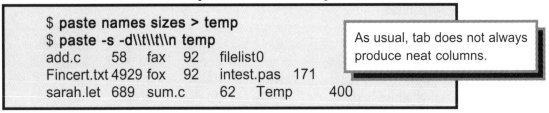

```
$ paste names sizes > temp
$ paste -s -d\\t\\t\\n temp
add.c        58    fax    92    filelist0
Fincert.txt 4929 fox    92    intest.pas   171
sarah.let   689  sum.c  62    Temp         400
```

As usual, tab does not always produce neat columns.

Alternatively, the two commands can be piped together:

> $ **paste names sizes | paste -s -d\\t\\t\\n -**

Note that dash at the end of the line. If you are piping into **paste**, the dash replaces the input filename. Whichever way you do it, the problem of uneven spacing means that the final result is not always as organised as you might like.

join – combine data files

This command is for use with relational databases – i.e. sets of files that are linked by a common key field. In a commercial environment, a typical database would be one to manage the stock. It would consist of two files. The first would hold the details for each stock line. e.g.

StockRef Description SupplierRef   QuantityInStock ...

The second would hold the supplier information:

SupplierRef   Name   Address1 Address2 ...

Splitting the data into two files is far more efficient that holding it all in one. A single stock file would have to hold the supplier's details for each stock line – and if a firm supplied a dozen lines, its name and address would appear a dozen times. Such duplication makes updating a real headache. If a supplier moved premises, someone would have to track down and alter every copy of the details. With the two file approach, a single correction is all that is needed.

SupplierRef is common to both files. With this as a key, you can produce a report that draws selected data from both. When reordering goods, you would pull the descriptions, references, quantities and prices from the first file, and the suppliers' details from the second.

To see how **join** works, you will need some suitable files. If you do not have any, create some with **cut** and **paste**. Each file should have at least two fields, one of which is common, and must be sorted into order of the key field. Files made up of cuts from your 'filelist' will do nicely. You should already have 'names', 'sizes' and 'dates'. Cut two more containing the permissions and the links (or any other).

```
$ cut -c-10 filelist > perms
$ cut -c11-12 filelist > links
```

paste them to make three new files. One with names, sizes and links; one with names and dates; one with links, sizes, names and permissions. The overlap of contents is intentional, as is the position of the 'names' field.

```
$ paste names sizes links > temp1        { names in field 1 }
$ paste names dates > temp2              { names in field 1 }
$ paste sizes names perms > temp3         { names in field 2 }
```

Now sort them into order by key field:

```
$ sort +0 -1 -o file1 temp1
$ sort +0 -1 -o file2 temp2
$ sort +1 -2 -o file3 temp3
```

If you don't tell it otherwise, **join** assumes that the key field is the first in each file, and that you want to include all the fields in the output.

```
$ join file1 file2
Fincert.txt 4929 1 Nov 28 17:29
Temp 400 1 Mar 18 1992
...
sarah.let 689 1 Nov 15 12:20
sum.c 62 1 Nov 10 14:05
```

You should be able to see that the fields are output in the order *name*, *size*, *links* and *date*. That is, the key field followed by the remaining fields of the first file then those of the second.

join options

-j Sets a **new key field**. Use this where the key is not the first field. The key is identified by the file and field number. For example, to join *file1* and *file3*, the name field must be identified in *file3*. If *file3* is listed second, its file number is 2. *name* is the second field – also 2. Thus:

```
$ join -j2 2 file1 file3
Fincert.txt 4929 1 4929 -rwx————
Temp 400 1 400 -rw-r—r—
...
sarah.let 689 1 689 -rw-r—r—
sum.c 62 1 62 -rw-r—r—
```

If we had given the files in the order 'file3 file1', the option would have read '-j1 2'. And note the punctuation in the -j option. There isn't any! The file and field numbers are simply separated by a space. If necessary, give the key field numbers for both files, including the -j with each.

If, for instance, the key field appeared in third place in the first file and sixth in the second, the command line would start:

```
$ join -j1 3 -j2 6
```

-o *list* Defines the **output** fields. You may have noticed that the *sizes* are given twice in that last output, as they were present in both input files. If you have duplication, or any other unwanted fields, you can refine the output by listing the fields which are to appear.

As with **-j**, the fields are identified by file and field number, but this time the numbers are separated by a dot. The order in which the fields are listed determined the order that they appear in the output.

For example, here is what we need to get fields from *file1* and *file3* in the order:

name (1.1), permissions (2.3), size (1.2) and links (1.3)

```
$join -j2 2 -o 1.1 2.3 1.2 1.3 file1 file3
Fincert.txt -rwx——— 4929 1
Temp -rw-r—r— 400 1
...
sarah.let -rw-r—r— 689 1
sum.c -rw-r—r— 62 1
```

-t*character* Defines *character* as the separator. The simple **join** assumes that the separators between fields in the input file will be spaces (any number of them), tab or newline, and it uses a single space as the separator in the output. Use this option to set an alternative character as the separator – noting that it will apply to both the input and output.

$ join -t: passlist grouplist

This would combine files where the separator was a colon.

join in pipes

join can only ever work on two files, though the first file can be replaced by input from the keyboard or a piped command. Within a pipe, **join** takes the form:

... *earlier command(s)* | join [options] - *file*

Note the dash to indicate input from the earlier command. It may replace either the first or second file.

Summary

❑ A **database** consists of a set of **records**, each of which contains data organised into **fields**. Directory listings and the /etc/passwd files are examples of databases in a Unix system.

❑ Data files can be **sorted into** alphabetical, numeric or date **order** with **sort**.

❑ **cut** will take a **vertical slice out of a file**. You could use this to extract all the values in a given field from a database.

❑ **paste** can be used to **combine files** that have been cut from a database. It can also be used to convert long narrow files so that they fit across the full width of the screen or printout.

❑ Where you have two or more data **files with a common key**, their data can be merged into a new file with **join**.

9 Shell programming

Shell scripts

Shell scripts are programs written in the shell's own language. They can be as complex as programs written in any other language, but a script does not have to be complex to be useful. A simple script may consist of a straightforward list of commands, and when it is executed, it has the same effect as if the commands had been given individually at the prompt. This is the sort we are interested in.

In this first example you will create a short file, consisting of one command, then pass it to **sh**, the (Bourne) shell program. This reads the script and executes any commands it finds.

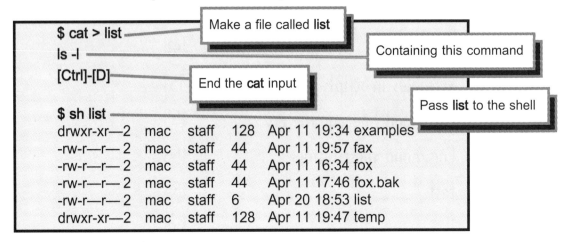

```
$ cat > list                    Make a file called list
ls -l                           Containing this command
[Ctrl]-[D]      End the cat input

$ sh list                       Pass list to the shell
drwxr-xr—2   mac   staff   128   Apr 11 19:34 examples
-rw-r—r— 2   mac   staff   44    Apr 11 19:57 fax
-rw-r—r— 2   mac   staff   44    Apr 11 16:34 fox
-rw-r—r— 2   mac   staff   44    Apr 11 17:46 fox.bak
-rw-r—r— 2   mac   staff   6     Apr 20 18:53 list
drwxr-xr—2   mac   staff   128   Apr 11 19:47 temp
```

This may seem a little pointless, as it takes longer to set up the script than it does to type the direct command. However, scripts makes good sense where you are regularly using a set of commands, or where a command line contains lengthy filenames.

Take note

This chapter applies to the Bourne shell only and ignores the C shell, for two reasons. First, Bourne shell scripts will run in any Unix environment, which C shell scripts will not. Second, there is scarcely room in this book to give a decent introduction to Bourne shell programming alone. It would be impossible to cover both adequately.

The following script will find the date, check the current path, then list files in date order. It needs three commands **date, pwd** and **ls -lt**. We'll use the initials to name the script 'dpl'.

```
$ cat >dpl
date
pwd
ls -lt
[Ctrl]-[D]
```

'**sh dpl**' will now find the date, current path and directory listing.

sh – A shell within a shell

```
$ sh dpl
```

This calls up a new invocation of the shell, which reads the script and interprets the commands. After the last one has been performed, the system exits back to the original shell. It does not normally matter that you are running a new shell to perform the script commands. It might if you were using variables, (see page 151), as usually these only have any meaning in the shell in which they were created.

The dot

The dot command (.) acts in much the same way as **sh**. The line:

```
$ . dpl
```

passes the 'dpl' script to the shell for execution, but this doesn't set up a new shell. As a result, existing variables are accessible to scripts activated by the dot. A limitation of this approach is that you cannot pass parameters to your script if it is run this way.

> ## Take note
>
> A shell program is referred to as a 'script', to emphasise that it is a text file, and to distinguish it from compiled programs.

Executable scripts

We can dispense with the **sh** command and run the script directly if we make it executable. And that is a lot easier than it sounds. All we need to do to make this executable is to change its permissions. Look closely at the file's listing as it is at the moment. If you create a text file, whether with **cat**, **vi**, or any other editor, it will normally have the permissions set so that you have read/write access and others have read-only access. Use the 'long list' version of **ls** to see the permissions:

```
$ ls -l dpl
-rw-r—r— 2 mac    staff    15 Apr 20 21:16 dpl
```

That **rw-** states that you can read and write the file, but not execute it. Change it to **rwx** with **chmod** to give yourself execute permission for the script, and check that the changes have been made:

```
$chmod u+x dpl
$ ls -l dpl
-rwxr—r— 2 mac    staff    15 Apr 20 21:16 dpl
```

You can now execute it by simply typing the name:

```
$ pdl
Fri Apr 25 12:45:36 GMT 1997
/usr/staff/mac
-rwxr—r—2  mac    staff   15    Apr 20 21:16 dpl
drwxr-xr— 2  mac    staff   128   Apr 11 19:34 examples
-rw-r—r— 2  mac    staff   44    Apr 11 19:57 fax
-rw-r—r— 2  mac    staff   44    Apr 11 16:34 fox
-rw-r—r— 2  mac    staff   44    Apr 11 17:46 fox.bak
-rw-r—r— 2  mac    staff   6     Apr 20 18:53 list
drwxr-xr—2  mac    staff   128   Apr 11 19:47 temp
```

Tip

If you want to try out the following examples, create the shorter scripts with a ›redirected cat, and use vi only for longer scripts or for editing existing ones. Run them with sh, as it is scarcely worth making them executable if they are only going to be used once or twice.

Variables in scripts

Variables were introduced back in Chapter 5. You will remember that a variable can be called by more or less any name you like, and that a value can be assigned to a variable by an expression of the type:

variable=value

In practice, there's limited use in assigning values to variables at the prompt. Variables play a more important role in shell scripts, where they can hold data entered by the user and pass it on to other programs or use it to control conditional branching. The command to collect a string of data from the keyboard is **read**.

You can see **read** at work in this example script.

```
echo Please enter your name:
read name
echo What day is it today?
read day
echo Hello $name Happy $day
```

Save this as **nameday**, then run it, and you will see something like this:

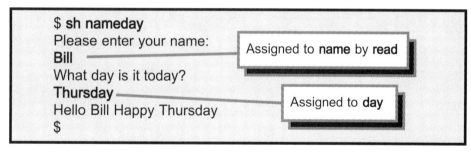

This is pointless but, as you will see below, by combining variables with a branching structure, you can create shell scripts that will act as menus to give easy access to a set of commands or programs.

Exporting variables

Variables normally only have meaning within the shell in which they are created, and scripts run in their own shell. If you want to pass variables, or changes to environmental variables, *down* to a script, they must be exported. (**export** does not allow you to pass variables back up to the previous shell.) Test export with these two scripts.

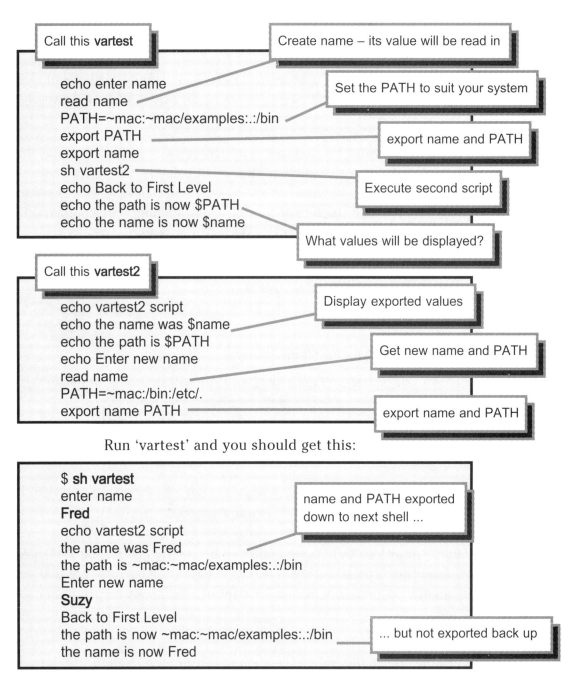

Call this **vartest**

Create name – its value will be read in

```
echo enter name
read name
PATH=~mac:~mac/examples:.:/bin
export PATH
export name
sh vartest2
echo Back to First Level
echo the path is now $PATH
echo the name is now $name
```

Set the PATH to suit your system

export name and PATH

Execute second script

What values will be displayed?

Call this **vartest2**

```
echo vartest2 script
echo the name was $name
echo the path is $PATH
echo Enter new name
read name
PATH=~mac:/bin:/etc/.
export name PATH
```

Display exported values

Get new name and PATH

export name and PATH

Run 'vartest' and you should get this:

```
$ sh vartest
enter name
Fred
echo vartest2 script
the name was Fred
the path is ~mac:~mac/examples:.:/bin
Enter new name
Suzy
Back to First Level
the path is now ~mac:~mac/examples:.:/bin
the name is now Fred
```

name and PATH exported down to next shell ...

... but not exported back up

The PATH and name were exported successfully from 'vartest' to 'vartest2', but the new values from there were not exported back. Edit 'vartest' to remove the **export** lines and run it again. You should find that 'vartest2' now has nothing for *name* and displays the default PATH.

Command line parameters

Also called **positional parameters**, these are a type of ready-made variable. When the shell scans a command line, any items written after the command are collected and stored in a set of variables numbered 1 to 9. These values can then be retrieved within the script by the expressions **$1, $2, $3,** etc. To see this, create the following script, calling it **params**.

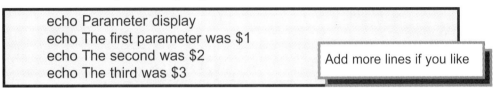

```
echo Parameter display
echo The first parameter was $1
echo The second was $2                    Add more lines if you like
echo The third was $3
```

Use **sh** to run the script, or make it executable with **chmod**. Don't try to run it with the dot command, as this cannot handle parameters. Whichever way you run it, type some words after the command.

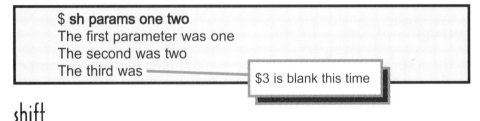

```
$ sh params one two
The first parameter was one
The second was two
The third was                    $3 is blank this time
```

shift

The shell command **shift** will move the parameter values along, so that $2 becomes $1, $3 becomes $2 and so on. The original $1 is lost in the process, of course. Edit your 'params' script to include **shift** as shown here, then run it again.

```
echo Parameter display with shifts
echo The first parameter was $1
shift
echo The second was $1
shift
echo The third was $1
```

Used in conjunction with some form of loop (see pages 161 and 165), **shift** provides a convenient way to work through a set of parameters.

How many parameters?

If you need to know how many command line parameters were entered, the number is recorded and held in the shell parameter #. You may also like to note that the asterisk * is equivalent to the whole set of command line parameters. Test them with this short script, 'paranum':

```
echo Parameter Counter
echo You entered $# items
echo They were $*
```

When run, you should see something like this:

```
$ sh paranum Tom Dick Harry
Parameter Counter
You entered 3 items
They were Tom Dick Harry
```

Comments in scripts

#, the hash, has a second and completely different meaning to the shell. Written by itself – without the preceding $ – it marks the start of a comment. When the shell runs through the script, it ignores # and anything written after it on the same line.

```
echo $thingy     # remind yourself what variables are used for
```

Comment lines can also be created by putting a colon (:) at the start. This must be treated with more care as the shell may try to interpret what follows the colon. To ensure that it is all ignored, enclose the comment in quotes. However you do them, comments are worthwhile.

```
: 'Comments make scripts more readable'
```

Take note

There are very few comments in the example programs in this chapter, as they have been replaced by more readable boxed comments.

Command substitution

A command – whether it is a system utility, application program or another script – written into a script is normally executed as if entered at the prompt. The process that is running the script is put on hold while the command is managed by a new process, within its own shell. Any output from the command is displayed on screen or sent to a file, but is not directly available to the script. With command substitution, this output can be captured.

If you enclose a command in grave accents (`` ` ``), then the shell runs that command and incorporates its output into the script. The resulting values can be passed to a variable or given to another command. In this script, for instance, command substitution is used to capture the current working directory in the variable 'start'. The directory is then changed, and a simple **pwd** is used to show that you are there. The 'start' value is later passed to **cd** to get you back to the original working directory.

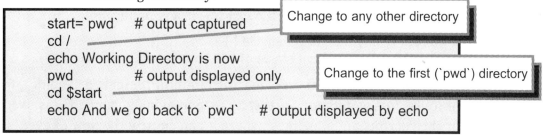

```
start=`pwd`    # output captured
cd /
echo Working Directory is now
pwd             # output displayed only
cd $start
echo And we go back to `pwd`    # output displayed by echo
```

Change to any other directory

Change to the first (`pwd`) directory

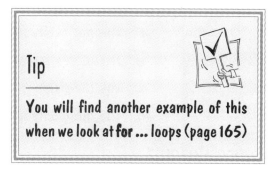

Tip

You will find another example of this when we look at for ... loops (page 165)

test

In Unix, almost all condition testing is handled by **test**. This is a utility program, not part of the shell programming language – though as you can run programs from within shell scripts, the distinction is largely academic. It can check the status of files as well as test the values held by variables. If true, the exit status is zero.

You can test in two ways:

    test *expression*   or just   **[*expression*]**

In the second form, the word **test** is omitted, and instead the expression is enclosed in [square brackets] – and note that you must leave spaces inside the brackets at both ends. The nature of the *expression* depends upon what you are testing.

Testing files

With files, there will be an initial option which defines the test. For example, **-f** will check that a file exists – as a plain file, not a directory.

```
$ test -f anyfile { or [ -f anyfile ] }
$ echo $?        { exit status of last command }
```

This will echo '0' to the screen if there is a file called 'anyfile'. In practice, you would not use **test** as a stand-alone command. It is used in shell scripts and pipelines, where it can control the flow of events.

These are the main file-testing options:

    -r   the file exists and you have read permission

    -w   the file exists and you have write permission

    -x   the file exists and you have execute permission

    -d   the file exists and is a directory

Testing strings

String values are tested using the operators = and != (not equal), and the expression is accompanied, as always, either by the **test** word or enclosed in [square brackets]. Take care with the punctuation. You must leave spaces around the operator. Quotes are only necessary around the strings if they contain spaces or special characters.

[$password = letmein]   { true if they are the same }
test $endflag != end   { true if they are different }

If you just wanted to check that a variable or parameter held a value – without caring what it was – then all you need is the identifier.

test $string

Testing numbers

Though command line parameters and variables are always strings, there are times when numerical testing is necessary. Some programs produce numeric values and all programs return an exit status to indicate success or failure. The operators here are abbreviations, rather than the symbols used in most other programming languages.

-eq   equal   -ne   not equal
-gt   greater than   -ge   greater or equal
-lt   less than   -le   less or equal

test $# -eq 4   { true if there were 4 command line parameters }

Compound expressions

Any number of simple expressions can be linked together using the operators ! (NOT), **-a** (AND) and **-o** (OR).

test ! -d $file   true if file is NOT a directory
test -f $file -a -r $file   true if a file AND readable
test $ans = y -o $ans = Y true if ans is either y OR Y

Where you have a combination of operators, operations can be enclosed in (curved brackets) so that they are evaluated first.

test ! ($ans = q -o $ans = Q)

This will give a true value if *ans* is neither 'q' nor 'Q'.

It is usually safer to use a series of simple tests rather than one complex expression. The shell can cope with either, but you will make fewer errors!

if

Like all programming languages, the shell has a set of words that can control the flow. It is a very limited set, but it contains enough to let you repeat actions, and to make the performance of an action dependent upon certain conditions.

With the **if** command you can test a value or file, and an action will be performed if the test proves true. At its simplest it takes the form:

```
if test expression
then
      action_if_true
fi
```

For example, to set up a greeting to your favourite user, try this:

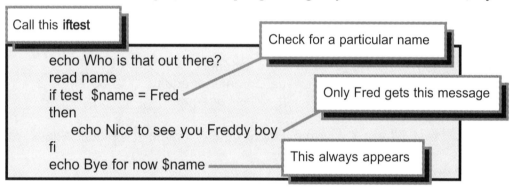

Call this **iftest**

Check for a particular name

```
echo Who is that out there?
read name
if test  $name = Fred
then
      echo Nice to see you Freddy boy
fi
echo Bye for now $name
```

Only Fred gets this message

This always appears

Run it, first with 'Fred' then with another name and you should see:

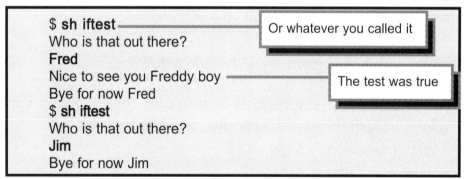

```
$ sh iftest
Who is that out there?
Fred
Nice to see you Freddy boy
Bye for now Fred
$ sh iftest
Who is that out there?
Jim
Bye for now Jim
```

Or whatever you called it

The test was true

This has only one action dependent upon the test, but there could be any number of commands between **then** and **fi**. These can be written one to a line, with no punctuation, or in a single line, punctuated by semi-colons.

elif and else

In a simple **if .. then ... fi** nothing special happens if the test proves false, and the flow moves on to the lines after the **fi**. If you want a false result to trigger an alternative action, then you need an **else** or **elif** (else if).

```
if test1
then
      action1
elif test2
   then
         action2
   else
      action3
fi
```

Tip

You can write the whole if ... fi statement on a single line, or break it over several lines to make it easier to read.

This next example is my general purpose utility called 'do'. Give it a filename and, depending upon the nature of the file, it will either change to a directory, run a program or pass it to **vi**. The program only performs the actions after a **then** if the preceding test is true, and having performed those actions, the flow leaps to 'Have a nice day'.

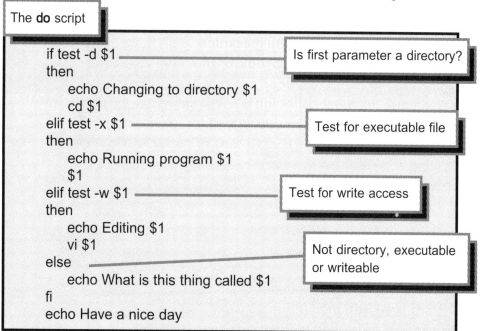

The **do** script

```
if test -d $1                          Is first parameter a directory?
then
      echo Changing to directory $1
      cd $1
elif test -x $1                        Test for executable file
then
      echo Running program $1
      $1
elif test -w $1                        Test for write access
then
      echo Editing $1
      vi $1                            Not directory, executable
else                                   or writeable
      echo What is this thing called $1
fi
echo Have a nice day
```

I suspect that the script needs some refinement to be truly usable!

Nested ifs...

if ... then ... else ... fi structures can be 'nested' inside one another, with the inner if only being brought into play if the test in the outer one proves true (or false – depending on where you slot it in).

The next script demonstrates multiple branches using nested **ifs**. It is a front end to **vi** that creates backup files and ensures that a filename is given when **vi** is invoked. The outer **if .. else ..** branches on the test of whether or not a filename is given; the inner **if .. else ...** divides the flow for new and existing files.

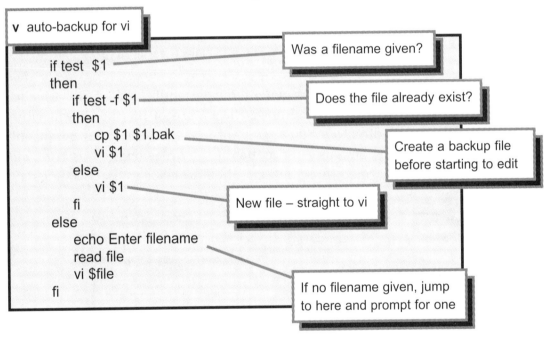

```
v  auto-backup for vi

        if test  $1                    Was a filename given?
        then
                if test -f $1           Does the file already exist?
                then
                        cp $1 $1.bak    Create a backup file
                        vi $1           before starting to edit
                else
                        vi $1
                fi                      New file – straight to vi
        else
                echo Enter filename
                read file
                vi $file                If no filename given, jump
        fi                              to here and prompt for one
```

while and until

We'll take these two together, for the structure is essentially the same. Like **if**, they produce conditional execution of a set of actions, but with these, the flow continues to repeat for as long as a particular condition is (or is not) met.

```
while test_is_true    or    until test_is_false
do
     actions
done
```

At the simplest, the **while** (**until**) word is followed directly by a test. If the test is true (false with **until**), the actions after **do** are performed and the flow loops back to the test line. In this first example, the script **shift**s through a set of command line parameters, stopping when it runs out of values.

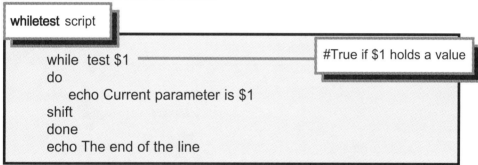

```
whiletest script

while  test $1 ————————————————— #True if $1 holds a value
do
     echo Current parameter is $1
shift
done
echo The end of the line
```

Run it, with a few items in the command line:

```
$ sh whiletest a b c
Current parameter a
Current parameter b
Current parameter c
The end of the line
```

You can write loops with a list of commands between **while** (**until**) and **do**. In these, the exit status of the last command in the list determines whether or not the *actions* after **do** are performed. The shape is then:

```
while                    or                   until
     actions
     do
          conditional_actions
done
```

The next script has a list of commands between **until** and **do**, with the last being a **test**. It keeps asking for a name and echoing a greeting until 'end' is entered. The structure behaves like the Pascal **repeat ... until** loop, but with a crucial difference. The actions after **do** – as well as the repetition of the loop – are conditional upon the test. In other languages a further branch command would be needed to handle this.

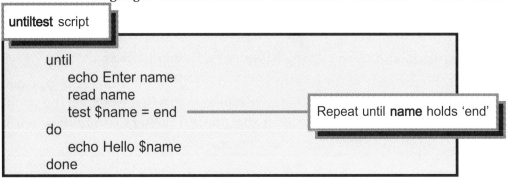

untiltest script

```
until
    echo Enter name
    read name
    test $name = end                    Repeat until name holds 'end'
do
    echo Hello $name
done
```

Run it and test it with a set of names:

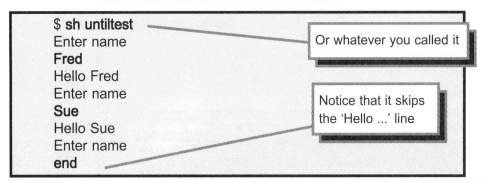

```
$ sh untiltest                          Or whatever you called it
Enter name
Fred
Hello Fred
Enter name                              Notice that it skips
Sue                                     the 'Hello ...' line
Hello Sue
Enter name
end
```

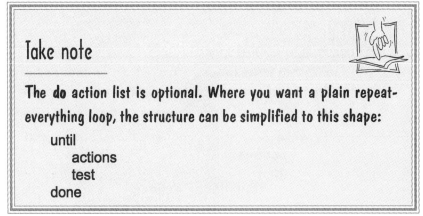

Take note

The **do** action list is optional. Where you want a plain repeat-everything loop, the structure can be simplified to this shape:

```
until
    actions
    test
done
```

case ... esac

The shell's **case** is the same as C's **case** and to Pascal's **switch ... case**. It causes the program to branch in one of a range of directions, depending upon the value that is held by a given variable. This offers a far neater method of dealing with a range of values than using a long series of **if** statements or a complex **if .. elif ...** structure. Use it to set up a menu-driven script – one where the user selects from a number of options by typing in a key word or character. The basic shape is:

```
case variable in
value1) action1 ;;          { single action ... }
value2) action2A            { or set of command lines }
        action2B
        ;;                  { marks the end of an option }
value3)                     { this generates no action }
esac
```

Note the punctuation carefully. There is a closing bracket after the value, and two semi-colons at the end of its related action(s). These are not needed on the last option before **esac**. The selector can be a single value or a set of alternative, separated by | bars, e.g. **q | Q)** might all select Quit.

Such a shell menu is often the neatest way to control a linked set of file-handling programs. You could also use one to give a friendly front-end to your system. Create this script and try it out:

Menu demonstration

```
echo User-friendly Unix!
until                                          Keep cycling through the menu
        echo List Directory .......... 1
        echo Change Directory ... 2
        echo Edit File ................. 3
        echo Remove File .......... 4
        echo Exit from Menu ....... 5
        read choice
        test $choice = 5
do
```

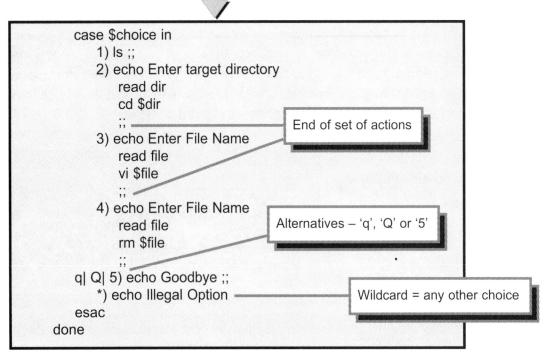

```
    case $choice in
        1) ls ;;
        2) echo Enter target directory
            read dir
            cd $dir
            ;;
        3) echo Enter File Name
            read file
            vi $file
            ;;
        4) echo Enter File Name
            read file
            rm $file
            ;;
    q| Q| 5) echo Goodbye ;;
        *) echo Illegal Option
    esac
done
```

End of set of actions

Alternatives – 'q', 'Q' or '5'

Wildcard = any other choice

The * in the last line is a standard shell wildcard and can therefore stand for anything. It traps any values that are not handled by the earlier case lines. Miss it out and the script will crash if an unknown value is entered.

for loops

In most programming languages, the **for** statement works through a set of numbers, performing the enclosed actions each time round the loop. The shell **for** runs through a set of *words*. Typically, the 'words' are filenames and the 'set' is a directory listing or the product of a wildcard expression. Here's its basic shape:

```
for variable [ in set ]
do
        actions
done
```

For example, the following will loop through a complete directory and display every readable file on screen.

```
for filevar in *
do
        if test -d $filevar
        then
            echo Directory: $filevar
        elif test -r $filevar
        then
            cat $filevar
        fi
done
```

> The * wildcard expands to create the directory listing

The set can come from the command line. This script will create a '.bak' copy of each file given in its command line.

backcopy script

> Nothing after the variable – no **in**, no **$1** – **for** reads from the command line without prompting

```
for filevar
do
    echo Copying $filevar to $filevar.bak
    cp $filevar $filevar.bak
done
```

Try it, feeding in a couple of files for which backup copies do not yet exist, then check the result by listing the '.bak' files.

```
$ sh backcopy memo1712 update.pas
Copying memo1712 to memo1712.bak
Copying update.pas to update.pas.bak
```

break and continue

These two shell commands provide ways of controlling the flow around **for**, **while** and **until** loops.

● **break** jumps out of a loop and back up to the previous level.

● **continue** jumps over the remaining looped lines and starts the next repetition from the top.

You can see them both at work in this example.

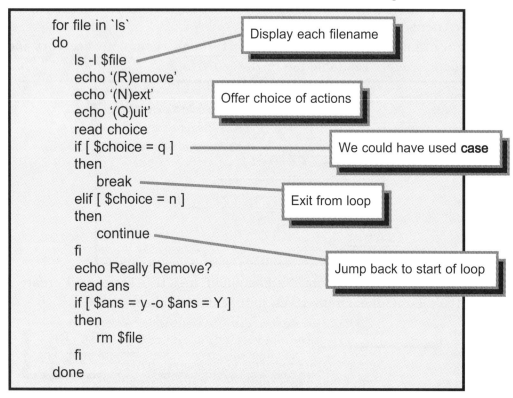

```
for file in `ls`
do
      ls -l $file
      echo '(R)emove'
      echo '(N)ext'
      echo '(Q)uit'
      read choice
      if [ $choice = q ]
      then
            break
      elif [ $choice = n ]
      then
            continue
      fi
      echo Really Remove?
      read ans
      if [ $ans = y -o $ans = Y ]
      then
            rm $file
      fi
done
```

Display each filename

Offer choice of actions

We could have used **case**

Exit from loop

Jump back to start of loop

Notice how command substitution is used to capture the directory listing in the first line of the script.

      for file in `ls`

The `ls` is expanded by the shell to provide a complete set of filenames.

exit [n]

exit closes down a script, and the shell that is running it. Give a number after the command to set your own exit status values. Miss it out and the exit status of the script will be that of the last command executed.

With more complex scripts, there may be several different reasons why they may fail. By marking each possible exit with a different value, the cause of failure can be identified.

```
....
if [ ! -f $name ]    # if name is not a file
then
    exit 2
elif [ ! -d $name ] # if name not a directory
then
    exit 3
fi
...
```

If you were running this script from within another, you could then test the exit status to determine what happens next.

Number values

The shell normally treats all values held in variables and parameters as strings of characters. This doesn't make number work impossible, but it does make it more difficult.

expr

expr evaluates expressions. Amongst other things, it can convert a string of digits into a numerical value, and perform simple arithmetic with integers (whole numbers). Using **expr** we can pass numbers as parameters, count the iterations of a loop or even calculate.

expr is a program, so to get values from it we use command substitution. For instance, to increment the value in a variable:

> count=`expr $count + 1`

If *count* had held '4' before this, it would hold '5' afterwards. Note those quotes. They are there to remind you that the variables are always held as strings of characters. **expr** will evaluate the string, calculate and pass the new value back – but it will still be a string once it is back in the variable.

The arithmetic operators that can be used with **expr** are:

+ addition	- subtraction	* multiplication
/ division	% remainder	

The backslash before the * is needed to prevent the shell from treating it as a wildcard.

The final script looks at a simple use of **expr**. It will print multiple copies of a file. Named 'mprint', its command line would take the form:

> mprint file number_of_copies

Within the script, the filename is the first parameter, $1, and the number is copied from $2 into the variable *count*. This will control the repetitions of the **while** loop. It is tested at the top by the expression:

> [count -gt 0]

As the **-gt** performs a numeric comparison, nothing more is needed here to get the number value from the variable.

At the end of the loop, the counter is decremented by the line:

count=`expr $count -1`

You might also notice the other two **test** expressions. At the top,

[! -f $1]

will produce a true value if a valid filename is not given. A few lines below, **if [$2]** makes sure that there is a second parameter. It is not necessary to check that the parameter holds a valid number at this stage, as the **while** test handles that. Note that you will probably need to change the line that does the printing, to suit your system.

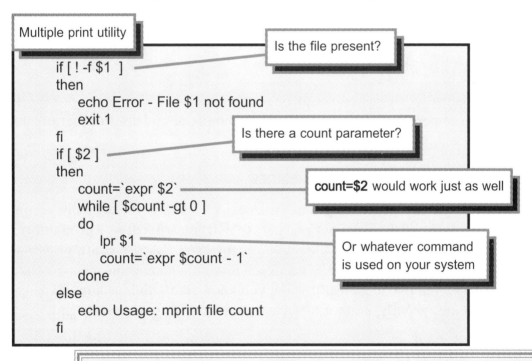

Multiple print utility

Is the file present?

Is there a count parameter?

count=$2 would work just as well

Or whatever command is used on your system

```
if [ ! -f $1 ]
then
     echo Error - File $1 not found
     exit 1
fi
if [ $2 ]
then
     count=`expr $2`
     while [ $count -gt 0 ]
     do
        lpr $1
        count=`expr $count - 1`
     done
else
     echo Usage: mprint file count
fi
```

Tip

Watch the spaces! They are crucial. There are no spaces around the '=' sign, that assigns the value to the variable. There are spaces between the values and operators that make up the arguments to the expr command.

Tips for shell programmers

Try and keep it simple

A script, like a Unix utility program, should do one job, but do it reliably. If more complex operations are needed, scripts can be linked in pipelines or called from within other scripts.

Make it readable

Use meaningful variable names and add comments wherever there may be any doubt about the effect of a line. Indent lines to bring out the structure. When you are debugging a script, it is much easier if you can glance down the side and see where loops start and end.

Don't reinvent the wheel

Before writing a new script, check the Reference Manual to see if there is something in that massive set of commands and utilities that will do the job.

Test everything before you use it in earnest

If you are processing files, run short test files through the script before you commit your real data to it. If you are writing a print utility, check the output on the screen before you risk the wrath of fellow users by clogging up the printer. If it is a file management script, that may remove files, test it when you know that a full backup has been done recently, so that files can be recovered if necessary.

Watch your scripts at work

Start up a new script with this:

```
$ sh -x script
```

The **-x** option will print out commands and their arguments as they are executed. You can then see exactly what your script is doing, as it does it.

Summaries

and summary

...modes of operation: **edit mode**, in which text can be moved,
...ed, deleted and corrected; **write mode**, where the only edit facility
...ut the characters that have just been written.

These pages give a summary of the keystrokes and a few of the **ed**-style
commands. If you use **vi** for programs and short texts, and a word-processor
for the heavier stuff, what is given here should be all you ever need.

Keystroke commands in edit mode

Switch to write mode:

a	Add after cursor	**i**	Inserting before cursor
o	Opening a new line below	**A**	Add at end of line
I	Insert at start of line	**O**	Open a new line above
R	Replace from cursor (Overwrite)		

Movement

h or [←]	Left one character	**j** or [↑]	Up a line
k or [↓]	Down a line	**l** or [→]	Right one character
w	Right one word	**b**	Left one word
0	Start of line	**$**	End of line
/string	Go on to *string*	**?string**	Go back to *string*
n	Repeat last / or ? search		

Editing

x	Delete character under cursor
X	Delete character left of cursor
dw	Delete word
dd	Delete line, copying text to buffer
yy	Yank – copy line to buffer
r	Replace character under cursor
~	Change case from upper to lower or vice versa
p	Paste line from buffer below cursor
J	Join current and next lines together

Repetition

. (dot)Repeat last edit operation

All movement and editing commands can be preceded by a number to give them multiple effect, e.g.

3x   Delete the next 3 characters

6yy   Yank 6 lines into the buffer

4p   Paste lines from the buffer 4 times

Other – but crucial

u   Undo the last edit operation

ZZ   Save and exit.

ed – style commands

In edit mode, press [:] to access these. The cursor will appear at the bottom of the screen.

:g/old/s//new/g Search for old and replace with new throughout

:q   Quit

:q!   Abandon edit and quit

:r *name*   Read file into text at cursor

:w *name*   Write text to file *name*

:*n1,n2* w *name* Write text from lines *n1* to *n2* to file *name*

Keystroke commands in write mode

^H   Delete character to left of cursor

^W   Delete word to left of cursor

Esc   Return to **edit mode**

Unix command summary

The summary concentrates on those commands and options that are likely to be of use or interest to ordinary users. It does not aim to meet the needs of advanced users, shell programmers or administrators.

Conventions used:

[item] optional item – control letter, filename, string or number

[item ..] optional item may be repeated any number of times

filespec one or more files, specified by a wildcard expression

Where no filenames are specified, input is from the standard input (keyboard), pipe or a redirected file; output is to the standard output (screen), pipe or a redirected file.

banner [string ..]

Creates large text for screen displays or printed headings. **banner** echoes the string to the screen in characters 8 rows high – or >redirects it to a file for printing. The text can be any length with these limitations: each string – either a single word or a set enclosed in quotes – may not have more than 10 characters; as each string is started on a new row, and you can only fit two full rows on screen, or five or six on a page.

cal [month] [year]

Gives a simple calendar for any month or year. As the year can be any value between 1 and 9999, it must be written in full. *Page 70.*

calendar

Scans a file called 'calendar' in the current directory and prints any messages linked to today's or tomorrow's dates. *Page 70.*

cancel [print-id]

Remove a file, identified by its *print-id* request identification, from the print queue. *Page 30.* See also **lp, lpstat**.

cat [-s] [-t] [-v] [file ..]

Concatenates and prints files. Files can be joined together by >redirecting the output to a new file, or joined to the end of existing files by >>append-redirection. *Page 114.*

Options

-s   Suppresses 'File Not Found' error messages.

-t   Prints tabs as '**^I**', but only when used with -v option.

-v   Non-printing characters are displayed in the form '**^X**'.

cd [directory]

Changes directory. If no directory is given, the change is to the user's Home directory. *Page 36.*

chmod

Changes the permission mode of a file or directory. *Page 66.*

chmod [ugoa] + - = [rwx] [file ..]

In symbolic mode permissions are set with letters.

The first letter identifies the class of user:

u	user/owner	**g**	other group members
o	any other user	**a**	all users

The operator is one of:

+	add	-	remove	=	set the access modes.

The second letter identifies the access mode being changed:

r	read	**w**	write
x	execute (file) or search (directory)		

chmod value [file ..]

In absolute mode the permissions are set in octal numbers.

The value is a 3-digit octal number. Each digit is the sum of the permissions set for the user, in the order: owner, group, others.

Permissions are valued: 4 = Read   2 = Write   1 = Execute,

e.g.

```
chmod 750 file  =     chmod u=rwx,g=rx file
```

175

cmp [-option ..] file1 file2

Compares two files, reporting the byte and line number at which differences are found. *Page 83.* See also **diff**.

Options

-l   Print the differing bytes as octal numbers.

-s   Suppress display of differences, and return exit status only.

The **exit status** is:

0   if the files are the same.

1   if they are different.

2   if a file cannot be found.

cp filespec [directory/][newfile]

Copies files within or between directories. When copying a single file to a new directory, the original name can be retained or a new name given. Sets of files, selected by wildcard expressions, may be copied in bulk into a different directory. *Page 43.* See also **mv**.

cpio

Copies selected files to and from an archive file, which may be on an external device (tape streamer or floppy disk). *Page110.*

    cpio -o[v]   { copy out to archive }

    cpio -i[dtv] [pattern ..] { copy in from archive }

Options

-o   Outward copying to archive.

-i   Inward copying from archive.

-d   (only with -i) Directories are created as needed.

-t   (only with -i) Creates a table of contents, without copying in.

-v   (both -o and -i) Lists files as they pass through.

When copying out, source files are usually piped from **ls** or **find** and >redirected to the archive file. Original pathnames are retained in full. When copying in, the archive is <redirected in, and files created in the current directory, or in other directories as specified by their pathnames. Files can be selected for copying by shell wildcard patterns.

crypt password [<input_file] [>output_file]

Encrypt or decrypt a text file, with encryption based on any chosen password. Files must be redirected <in and >out from **crypt**. Give **crypt** a password and a text file and to produce an encrypted file. Give it the same password and the encrypted file to get your clear text back again.

```
$ crypt enigma <myfile >mysecret
$ rm myfile
```

This has encrypted *myfile* with 'enigma' as the password, and then removed it so that only the coded version remains.

```
$ crypt enigma <mysecret
```

This will decode the file and output it to the screen.

csh [-options] [script]

Invokes a new C shell, and executes a script if given. *Page 84.*

csplit [-option ..] filename [argument ..]

Splits files into blocks, based on text items or line numbers. Each section ends on the line before the next text or number argument. The new filenames are made up of '**xx**..', followed by a two-digit number. *Page 121.* See also **split**.

Options

-s   Suppress the character count as files are created.

-k   Keep files created so far if a bad argument stops the command.

-f *base*   File names will start with *base* instead of **xx**.

Arguments

/pattern/   Write a file for the section up to *pattern*.

%pattern%   Skip the section up to *pattern*.

number   Section ends at line *number*-1.

cut

Cuts fields from a data file, with fields specified by field number or character position. Input files are omitted when used in a pipe; output is to a >redirected file or the next command in a pipe. *Page 136.* See also **join, paste**.

```
cut -clist [file ..]              { character positions }
cut -flist [-option ..] [ file ..]    { field numbers }
```

Options

-c*list*   *list* is a set of ranges separated by commas, e.g. 3-9,15-20. If the start or end is missing, the start (end) of line is assumed.

-f*list*   *list* is a set of numbers, counting from 1 as the first field.

-d*char*   Set the *char*acter to be used as the field delimiter, instead of space.

-s   Suppresses the output of lines with no delimiters. These might be headings for tables.

date

Returns today's date and time. *Page14.*

dc [file]

Desk calculator (reverse Polish notation). Normally used interactively, but a command sequence can be passed in from a file. *Page 68.*

dc recognises the operators:

    + - * / % (remainder) ^ (exponentiation) v (square root)

The key commands are:

p   print the value at the top of the stack.

q   quit.

diff file1 file2

Compares two files and reports on their differences. The report is in the form of a set of lines showing the commands that would have to be given to **ed** to make the files identical. Unless you are into **ed**, the exit status is probably the most useful feature of this. See also **cmp**.

The **Exit status** is:

0   if the files are identical.

1   if they are different.

2   indicates problems.

echo [argument ..]

Output text or variable contents to the screen. Intended for use within shell scripts, to prompt the user or to indicate the progress of the script. *Page 77.*

egrep [option ..] expression file

Extended version of the **grep** command, that can handle more complex search expressions. *Page 107.* See also **fgrep**, **grep**.

expr argument

Evaluate an expression to give an integer value. Used to get numerical values out of variables, and perform calculations in scripts. *Page 168.*

An argument is a variable name alone or variables and/or values linked by an operator from the set:

+ - * (multiply) / %

NB. The * (for multiply) must be escaped by a backslash. In scripts, the command must be enclosed in `grave accents` to obtain the resulting value.

fgrep [option ..] pattern .. file

Fast version of **grep**, which gains its speed by only handling strings, without wildcards or other symbols. *Page 107.* See also **egrep**, **grep**.

file [-f listfile] filespec

Takes an educated guess at the nature of a file, or set of files specified by a wildcard expression. *Page 49.*

Option

-f *listfile* The files to be checked are specified in *listfile*.

find startpoint expression [action]

Searches through all the directories, below a given startpoint, for files that meet certain criteria. A search is typically by name, type or time of last access or change. The names of found files can be output to the screen, a file or down a pipe. Files may also be passed directly to a command for copying, removal or other processing. *Page 96.*

Options

-atime *number*	Files accessed since the *number* of days.
-cpio *device/file*	Copies files to the *device* or *file*.
-ctime *number*	Files changed since the *number* of days.

-depth	Work upwards from the lowest directory.
-exec *command*	Perform the *command*. Empty curly brackets {} take the place of the filename in the *command*.
-name *filespec*	Files matching the name or a wildcard pattern.
-print	Prints the filenames on the standard output.
-type *char*	The *char* codes are:

             b - block special **c** - character special

             d - directory   **f** - plain file   **p** - pipe

The *expression* can be a single option and parameter, or several in brackets.

grep [options] pattern [files]

Searches through files for matches to a specified pattern, printing out any lines that contain matching text. *Page 101.* See also **egrep**, **fgrep**.

Options

-c	Only print a count of the number of matches.
-f *file*	Take the search patterns from the *file*.
-i	Ignore upper-lower case distinctions.
-l	List the names of the files with matches.
-n	Give the line number of each match.
-s	Suppress error messages for missing files.

Patterns

The search patterns are a combination of text and symbols. The key ones are:

.	standing for any character.
*	any number of repeated characters.
[*chars*]	any one of the bracketed characters.
^	pattern at the start of a line.
$	pattern at the end of a line.

Patterns containing spaces or symbols, must be enclosed in quotes.

The files can be specified in the command line, or piped through from a previous command.

join [options] file1 file2

Joins together the lines (records) from two datafiles that have a common field. The files must both be sorted into order on the common field. By default, this is the first in each line, and fields are separated by spaces, tab or newline. Each output line normally has the common field, then the remaining fields of the first file, followed by the remaining fields of the second file. *Page 143*. See also **cut**, **paste**.

Options

-j*filenum field* Identifies an alternative field as the common field. Fields are counted from 1. If *filenum* is missing, the *field* number applies to both files.

-o *list* The *list* defines the fields to be output, with fields identified by number, in the form *file.field*, and separated by commas. e.g. 2.3, 1.4

-t*char* Sets *char* as the field separator.

kill [-9] PID

Closes down a process – especially useful with those that refuse to respond to less drastic measures. Unless the process is running in the background, you will have to kill it from another terminal. You will probably need to use **ps** to find the PID (Process IDentification number). *Page 16*. See also **ps**.

The **-9** option defines the signal number to be sent to kill the process. Though not essential, it does guarantee success.

ln -s path/filename path/linkname

Creates a new symbolic link to an existing file, so that it can be accessed from another directory. The directory can be in another (user's) area on the same or a different file system. The linked file may be identified by the same or a different name. *Page 66*.

When **rm** is used on a linked file, it only removes the link. This applies in the original directory as elsewhere. The file is only removed with the last link.

The **-s** identifies this as a symbolic link.

As linked files can cause problems when backing up, on some installations, the use of this command may be restricted to the superuser.

lp [option ..] files

The main printing command, probably replaced in practice by a locally-written shell script that gives better control of the system's printers. *Page 29.* See also **cancel**, **lpstat**

Options

-c   Make temporary copies of the files before printing. The files can then be deleted or edited without affecting the printout. The temporary files are removed by the system.

-d*device*   The *device* selects an alternative to the default printer.

-n*number*   Print that *number* of copies of each file in the list.

-t*title*   Print the *title* on the leading (banner) page.

lpstat [option ..]

Prints information about the status of line printer(s). Options specify the nature of the information to be given. Without options, it prints the current status of the user's print requests only. *Page 30.* See also **cancel**, **lp**.

Options

-d   The default destination for **lp**.

-o*[list]*   The status of output requests. The optional *list* specifies printers, request-ids or a mixture of both.

-t   Total status information.

Other options cover aspects of the system's printers and print scheduler.

ls [-options] [path/][filespecification]

Scans a directory and lists the names of files in it. Options control the layout and order of the list, the amount of information about the files, and the depth of the scan. If no path is given, the current directory is assumed; if no wildcard file specification is given, then all files – apart from those starting with . (dot) are shown. *Page 37.*

Options

-a   All files, including those starting with . (dot).

-C   Column layout, with names sorted down the screen.

-F	Show filetype, marking directories with / and executable files with *.
-l	Long listing, showing permissions, ownership, size and date.
-q	Use **?** in place of any non-printing characters in names.
-r	Reverse order of listing.
-R	Recursive listing, giving the contents of each sub-directory.
-t	List in time order, newest files first.
-x	Column layout, with names sorted across the screen.

mail [options]

Read messages in your mailbox. *Page 61.*

Options

-r	Read mail in reverse order, oldest message first.
-t	When sending mail, this attaches to the message a list of all users who will receive copies.

When **reading mail**, use these keystroke commands:

+ -	Go to next or previous message.
d	Delete the current message.
s *file*	Save the current message as *file*.
*	Display a summary of commands.
q	Quit.

mail users [<message_file]

Send mail to other users on the system. Write the message directly after giving the command, ending with [Ctrl]-[D], or redirect an existing message file in the command line.

Your system may well have a more user-friendly alternative to **mail**.

man command

On-line help utility that prints entries from the User's Reference Manual. *Page 54.*

mkdir directory_name(s)

Make a new directory. *Page 41.*

Directory names can be up to 14 characters long (but see page 108). The name may not include any spaces or the symbols:

> * . ? : ; ! " ' [ ] ( ) \

mesg [y,n]

Open (**mesg y**) or close (**mesg n**) others' access to your terminal for messaging. *Page 64.* See also **who**, **write**.

mv filespec directory[newfile]

Move a file, or set of files to a new directory. Files can be moved in bulk using wildcard expressions, and retain their original names. *Page 48.* See also **cp**.

mv oldfile [path/]newfile

Renames a file. If a file already exists with the *newfile* name, it will be overwritten. Only one file can be renamed at a time.

pack [-f] filespecification

Compresses a file or set of files. The originals are removed and replaced by the packed versions, marked by a **.z** suffix. Packing has most effect with simple text files. The smaller the range of characters, the greater the saving. The packing process has overheads, and with small files these can outweigh the gains. **pack** does a before-and-after comparison and will normally abandon the attempt if it is not worth while. *Page 108.* See Also **pcat**, **unpack**.

Option

-f   Forces a file to be packed, whether or not it is worth the effort.

passwd

Changes your password. For security reasons, **passwd** asks you to type your old password before allowing you to change it. If you have forgotten your old password, see your system administrator. The superuser can change any password without having to type in the current text. *Page 15.*

paste [-s] [-dlist] file1 file2 ..

Merges two or more files in columns. As a tab separates one item from the next, columns are irregular if items vary in length. *Page 140.* See also **cut**, **join**.

Options

-s   **paste** a long, narrow file into columns. If there are several files, they will be pasted in sequence, not in parallel columns.

-d*list*   *list* is a set of separators to be used in place of the normal tabs and newline, after the item from the last file. The separators are used in sequence, cycling back to the start if needed.

If one of the files is to be replaced by data piped from another command, indicate it with a dash (-) in the command line.

pcat file ..

The equivalent of **cat** for packed files. *Page 109.* See also **pack**, **unpack**.

pg [option ..] [file]

Displays a file or the output from a pipe a screenful at a time. *Page118.*

Options

-p *string*   Set alternative prompt string.

-c   Clear the screen before each new page.

-s   Display messages in standout mode.

+*line*   Start the display at *line* number.

+/*pattern*/   Start the display at the **grep**-style pattern.

When **pg** is running, use these commands:

[+/-]*num*   Go to page *num* or forward (+) or back (-) *num* pages.

[+/-]*num* l   (Letter 'l') Go forward or back *num* lines.

[+/-]*num* d   Go forward or back *num* half-pages.

[n]/*pattern*/   Display from the next or the *n*thline containing a match.

[n]?*pattern*?   As above, searching backwards.

s *name*   Save the current file under the *name*.

h   Help. Display the commands.

q   Quit.

ps [-f]

Reports the status of your current processes. *Page 16.*

Options

-f   Gives full information about the process, rather than the normal user name, terminal, running time and command name.

pwd

Displays the path to the working (current) directory. *Page 12.*

rm [-options] filespecification

Permanently removes a file or set of files. *Page 47.*

Options

-f   Forces removal without any check.

-i   Interactive – each file is presented for confirmation before removal.

-r   Recursively deletes the contents then the directory itself.

rmdir directory

Permanently removes a directory. The directory must be emptied before it can be removed. *Page 41.* See also **rm**.

sh [-options] [script]

Invokes a new Bourne shell, within the current one, and executes a script if given. These start-up options may be useful when testing scripts. *Page 76.*

Options

-e   Exit from the shell if a command fails

-n   Read commands but do not execute them

-v   Display lines as they are read

-x   Display commands and their arguments as they are processed

Other options are available. See the Manual.

sleep seconds

Does nothing for a set time. Mainly used for creating a pause in a shell script, or run in the background with an **echo** to give a timed reminder. *Page 71.*

sort [-option ..] [field ..] [file ..]

Sorts the lines of a file into order on the basis of one or more key fields. The sort may be in ASCII, dictionary, month or numeric order. Can also merge – into order – two or more sorted files with the same record structure. Unless otherwise specified, the sort takes the whole line as the 'key field'. *Page 132.*

Options

-c	Check if the file is in the given order, and do nothing if it is.
-m	Merge two ready-sorted files.
-u	Unique lines – do not repeat lines with the same keys.
-o*outfile*	Send to *outfile* rather than the standard output.
-d	Dictionary order
-f	Fold lower to upper case
-M	Month order
-n	Numeric order
-r	Reverse order – can be combined with any of the above
-t*char*	Sets alternative *char* as the field separator.

Key field specification

A sort may be based on several keys, and each key may extend across several adjacent fields. Fields are counted from 0 on the left. Keys are defined in the form **+***start* **-***end*, where *start* is the first field to include and *end* is the next field after the key. e.g. +2 -4 sets fields 2 and 3 to be used together as the key.

If an input file is to be replaced by data piped from another command, indicate it with a dash (-) in the command line.

spell [-option ..] file

Spell-checks a file, outputting a list of unrecognised words. *Page 126.*

Options

-b	Use British, not US, spelling.
+*file*	Include your own list of specialised words, stored in *file*.

split [-num] file [basename]

Split a large file into sections, each of 1000 lines, or other length if specified.

The new files will be named 'aa' through to 'zz', or will have those letters appended to a basename, if given. *Page 121.*

-num Sets the size of each section in number of lines.

stty

Sets the options for a terminal. Rarely required by the ordinary user, partly because the terminals may well have a simpler means of setting options built into their hardware, mainly because your system administrator should have set the terminals for optimum performance, and anything you do is likely to make things worse.

Options

Many and various. See the Manual.

tail [option ..] file

Display the last part – 10 lines by default – of a file. *Page 117.*

Options

+/-num[lbc] Sets the place from which to start the display, counting from the start (+) or end (-) of the file.

The count can be in **l**ines, **c**haracters or **b**locks.

tee [-a] filename

Send output to a named file as well as to the standard output. *Page 58.*

Option

-a Append to the named file.

test -option file

Tests the status of a file. *Page 156.*

Options

-d	Directory	**-f**	File, not directory
-r	Read permission	**-w**	Write permission
-x	Execute permission	**-s**	File size greater than 0

test expression

Tests the value in a variable. The **test** command word can be replaced by [
] around the expression, but the brackets must be separated from the
expression by spaces.

The nature of the expression depends upon what is being tested.

Valid expressions

-z *string*	String of 0 characters
-n *string*	String of 1 or more characters
string1 = *string2*	Strings are the same
string1 != *string2*	Strings are NOT the same

test num1 -operator num2

Tests the value in a variable.

Operators

-eq	equal	-ne	not equal
-gt	greater than	-lt	less than
-ge	greater or equal	-le	less or equal

time command

Reports on the time it took for a command to execute, giving three values.
Page 71.

real	total elapsed time.
user	processor time.
sys	time elsewhere in the system.

umask *nnn*

Sets the access modes for new files. *Page 76.* See also **chmod**.

nnn is a 3-digit octal number that will be subtracted from 777 to give the
permissions for a new file.

unpack file

Restores to normal a file packed by **pack.** *Page109*. See also **pack**, **pcat**.

wc [-options] file

Counts the word, lines and characters in text files. *Page 125.*

Options

-l count lines

-**w** count words

-**c** count characters

who [-options]

Shows the names, terminal ID and start time for those users who are currently logged on to the system. *Page 14.* See also **mesg**, **write**.

The special version **who am i** gives the name of the user logged on at the current terminal.

Options

-**H** Print headings above the columns

-**q** Quick version – gives only the names

-**T** Also reports the terminal status. + shows that the terminal is open for others to **write** to; - shows that it is not open.

write user

Interactive messaging utility, copying input from your keyboard to another user's screen. The connection holds until [Ctrl]-[D] is entered. *Page 64.* See also **mesg**, **who**.

write can only be used if the other user is open to receive messages.

Index

194